When Your Job Sucks

Postmodern Wage Slave Narratives

Dust Cover

When Your Job Sucks, the prime steakhouses of the world and hipster health-food eateries are closed to you. Therefore, within this litany of job descriptions, that are hopefully worse than yours, the reader will find cheap-eating leads in the form of The Poor Tour and The Ghetto Gourmet, the author's own answer to eating on less a week than most spend on their Saturday night dinner tip.

A Punch Buggy Book
Copyright 2016 James LaFond

Books by James LaFond

Nonfiction
The Fighting Edge, 2000
The Logic of Steel, 2001
The First Boxers, 2011
The Gods of Boxing, 2011
All Power Fighting, 2011
When You're Food, 2011
The Lesser Angles of Our Nature, 2012
The Logic of Force, 2012
The Greatest Boxer, 2012
Take Me to Your Breeder, 2014
The Streets Have Eyes, 2014
Panhandler Nation, 2014
The Ghetto Grocer, 2014
American Fist, 2014
Don't Get Boned, 2014
Alienation Nation, 2014

When Your Job Sucks

In The Chinks of The Machine, 2014
How the Ghetto Got My Soul, 2014
Saving the World Sucks, 2014
Taboo You, 2014
Winter of a Fighting Life, 2014
Narco Night Train, 2014
Into the Mountains of Madness: in [3 volumes], 2014
Incubus of Your Sacred Emasculation, 2014
Breeder's Digest, 2014
The Third Eye, 2015
Modern Agonistics, 2015
By the Wine Dark Sea, 2015
The Pale Usher, 2016
The End of Masculine Time, 2015
War Drums, 2015
A Thousand Years in His Soul: The Poets, 2015
A Thousand Years in His Soul: The Seers, 2015
Of Lions and Men, 2015
Your Trojan Whorse, 2016
On Bitches, 2016
Equidistant Drowning Babies, 2015
The Boned Zone, 2015
A Sickness of the Heart: Part One, 2015
Let the Weak Fall, 2015
If I Were King, 2015
Dark Art of an Aryan Mystic, 2015
Welcome to Harm City: White Boy, 2015
When You're Food: Raw, 2016
The Punishing Art, 2016
Twerps, Goons and Meatshields, 2016
Our Captain, 2016
Stillbirth of A Nation, 2016
America in Chains, 2106
40,000 Years from Home, 2016
The Sardonyx Stone, 2017
Neanderthal Resistance, 2016
Habitat Hoodrat: Ho Nation, 2016
When Your Job Sucks, 2016
A Once Great Medieval City, 2016
Right on White Time, 2016
A Well of Heroes: One, 2016
A Well of Heroes: Two, 2016
Paleface Sunset, 2016
Thriving in Bad Places, 2016
Into Wicked Company, 2016

Under The God of Things, 2016
One Soul Under God, 2016
Dawn in Dindustan, 2016
When Your Job Sucks, 2016
Good Morning, Dindustan! 2016
Habitat Hoodrat: Yo Nation, 2016
The Combat Space, 2017
A Dread Grace: One, 2017
The Liver-Eater Reader, 2017
Lunch at Café Dindustan, 2017
In Words, 2017
Slave Nation, 2017
Why Grownups Suck, 2017
A Dread Grace: Two, 2017
A Well of Heroes: Three, 2017
The Boxer Dread, 2017

Fiction
Astride the Chariot of Night, 2014
Sacrifix, 2014
Rise, 2014
Motherworld, 2014
Planet Buzzkill, 2014
Fruit of The Deceiver, 2014
Forty Hands of Night, 2014
Black and Pale, 2014
Daughters of Moros, 2014
Darkly, 2014
This Design is Called Paisley, 2015
Hurt Stoker, 2015
Poet, 2016
Triumph, 2015
Winter, 2015
The Spiral Case, 2016
Hemavore, with S. L. James, 2016
Yusuf of the Dusk, 2016
Beyond the Pale, 2017
RetroGenesis: Day 1, with Erique Watson, 2015
Easy Chair, 2015
Happily Ever Under, 2015
Road Killing, 2015
Fat Girl Dancing, 2015
Buzz Bunny, 2015
T. Spoone Slickens, Inquire, 2015

Dream Flower, 2015
The Song of Jeannot, 2015
Organa, 2015
A Hoodrat Halloween, 2015
Buzz Bunny, 2015
The Consultant, 2015
Reverent Chandler, 2015
He, 2016
Little Feet Going Nowhere, 2016
DoomFawn, 2016
The Jericho Bone, 2016
Ire and Ice, 2016
Night City, 2016
Night Song of the Nords, 2016
The Absolvant, 2017
Kettle of Bones, 2017
Wendigo, 2017
Sold, 2017

Sunset Saga Novels
Big Water Blood Song, 2011
Ghosts of the Sunset World, 2011
Beyond the Ember Star, 2012
Comes the Six Winter Night, 2012
Thunder-Boy, 2012
The World is Our Widow, 2013
Behind the Sunset Veil, 2013
Den of The Ender, 2013
God's Picture Maker, 2014
Out of Time, 2015
Seven Moons Deep, 2016
WhiteSkyCanoe, 2017

Contents

For Larry, the quintessential NCO of grocery managers—just one more tour to go, Boss!

The Poor Tour

When Your Job Really Sucks
You Live in the Ghetto and Eat and Drink at Cheap Joints

© 2016 James LaFond

The When Your Job Sucks stories just keep barreling in. I get as much of this stuff as violence and envision the project as an ongoing series to be collected annually. Two naturally related projects are The Poor Tour and the Ghetto Gourmet, both going at a slow pace, since I usually engage in eating out when pressed for writing time and try my hand at the microwave and crockpot recipes while editing and publishing books.

Hence the amalgamated theme of living the low life, with all three uplifting aspects of postmodern urban life for the rat race dropout dovetailing into a white trash literary trilogy, between the two covers of the same affordable book.

Looking for Crazy Mark
A Rainy Walk Down A Soot-stained Memory Lane

© 2015 James LaFond

On Tuesday evening of June second I took a walk down Belair Road from the city line, attempting to establish some intelligence on Crazy Mark. I was nervous, not having been in contact with anybody local other than Ron, Sol, Chuck or Aldo for five years, and not having much familiarity with the hoodrat tribe on that north-south axis, which runs parallel to Harford Road, the axis I live on two miles to the west.

My first order of business would be to look for familiar faces on the street and in bars, headed down the left side of the road. If I find no one I know, I might be able to strike up an acquaintance with someone who might know Mark. Mark never patronized bars, but people know him on sight, and the white guys that still drink in these bars would be about our age and work in the trades. Since he was stripping copper out of houses in this area maybe some of these guys had had an encounter or sighting. This is phase one, a one-mile barhop that will basically map the urban blight and demographic tilt.

I was out from 6:30 to 9:30, getting home at about 10:00.

Buck Fowler's Tavern

This is a narrow linear bar with small tables to the back, seating a total of 30.

All the patrons were white men from 50 to 70. One was a drinker, two played poker machines, and six were engaged in a shuffle bowl game in the back.

The barmaid was a pleasing brunette in a football jersey of about 40, who was enjoying the music on the juke box and playing shuffle bowl. The music was Tom Petty, Great Train Robbery and Skynard.

The tap beer was limited to Bud and Coors light. It is a predominantly bottled beer joint with my 8 ounce Rollin Rock costing $3.50.

The beer and drink selection is calibrated not to appeal to blacks or young people.

There are two TV monitors with the news on.

I knew none of these men.

The Coach House Inn

Half of this sprawling white trash bar has been rented to a guy who runs a burger stand and does more business than the bar. There is a back area for smoking and sitting outside under an awning, which is reserved for the bar patrons.

The bar itself is a square room around a central pillar or boxed in staircase in three sections: the far section having two pool tables from where the deck is accessed, the small table seating area with three high three-seat tables, and the bar at the front door, a small 13 seat rectangle with a bottle beer cooler under a large screen TV.

The barmaid is a very good looking and well dressed small girl of 50. This girl is the classiest barmaid I've seen in a dive like this forever, making me wonder if she owns it.

There are nine patrons, all white working class guys in the trades ranging in age from 35-55. Four play pool and smoke on the deck while five sit at the bar.

I order a shot of Petron, as there is no draft. Keeping draft out of your bar pretty much prohibits a black male clientele. There are also no forties, no malt liquor, and no fortified wine in the case. The Patron sets me back $8!

I don't know any of these guys, although I can see how it would be easy to engage them in the future, as the news on TV starts up some conversation. These are not the "let's forget and be merry" crowd up the street where I just left.

Bird Land Sports Bar and Grill

A gentrification attempt at a mixed race sports bar, complete with curb to door awning and a towering painting of celebrity football felon Ray Lewis screaming his African American angst, has been closed for some years now.

Mixers

This bar has changed hands for decades, closed between owners as often as not. I can tell by the neighborhood and the exterior that this is a mixed drink bar for older black guys who do not want to have to deal with young thugs or the wife. I will find no news of Crazy Mark here, but will stop back sometime.

The Hub

This was Ricks' bar when I moved to town in 1981. I worked with a black guy who shot the place up and did time after the redneck patrons chased him out for coming in with a white girl. He was a nice guy.

Rick's son eventually got in a fight with another white trash guy from Waverly and got his nose bit off. Soon after the bar changed hands.

From 1995-2012 it was owned as the Hubcap by a retired city cop, who was a real asshole, but a good bar owner. He fed cops breakfast for free and kept a good kitchen. I would eat breakfast there often. He had a huge selection of movies that the patrons would enjoy and discuss, and a pool table in the back. A guy I knew was murdered behind this bar by three dudes who never even got charged, his head smashed in with the concrete end of a pulled up fence post

The bar has now been bought by a Pakistani family who has also bought the VFW lodge across the street! I will check that out on my next jaunt.

The kitchen has been replaced by a ghetto carry out six-pack and liquor selection with its own separate counter and clerk.

The barmaid is amber, with amber skin, amber hair, and a curvy body seemingly designed by a God who wanted to wow black guys across the color line. She dresses like a slut, dances behind the bar for tips, and slings booze like a pro. I'd say she's a well worn 30. Behind the bar with her is a Pakistani security guard—the kind with a baggy khaki shirt long enough to conceal a tulwar or an AK-47.

Outside stand three brown men of undetermined race who work for the bar in some capacity and seem to have quit for the day.

The bar is long dark and narrow, with the package goods side long and well lit. There is a good selection of bottle and tap beer as well as rail drinks.

In the front sits a fat white man of 50, a good looking white woman of 30, a pretty black girl of 30, a skinny white guy of 35, and, all the way to the back and filling the rest of the 20 bar stools are 16 black guys, mostly in their 20s shouting at each other as rap music blares so loud that I decide not to get a drink

I recognize no one.

As I select a six pack of Resurrection ale to take over to Chuck's house, who is one of three friends who live in the area, I notice that the nighttime security man is coming on duty, a six foot five inch 280 pound wall of Caucasian muscle armed with a nine millimeter and a flashlight, who Chuck later tells me searches everyone who enters for weapons. When you get here, to the point where a neighborhood package goods and bar needs to have what is essentially a paramilitary presence to stay open, then you have hit the hard ghetto. You are in the hood, right in The Boned Zone where every midsized city neighborhood with a majority black population holds on, before either weathering the storm, or blighting out.

Consider that these 16 loud young black men are most likely working guys, who have sought a much safer drinking venue than is normally available in majority black neighborhoods. I may not like their music or their manners, but they were friendly enough, and have actually sought out the protection of a Pakistani merchant clan, who have hired a guy who looks like he was designed at Black Water, to keep them all alive and attached to their wallet while they unwind from the day and party into the night.

Chuck's House

Having had enough, and honestly not feeling up to finding out what the Garden Inn has turned into down the road, I head over to Chuck's for a beer, and then head home in a misty rain with my head on a swivel.

As I look for Crazy Mark and anyone who might know of his whereabouts I'll file a report on the rest of the bars along the remaining four miles of this five mile stretch of blighted urban road. I'm a mile in and it's already looking grim.

WTF?

A Former Visitor to Baltimore Suggests a Non-fiction Serial

© 2015 James LaFond

Haven't been by your web site yet but hopefully you have a Harm City recap on any shenanigans you witnessed this 4th of July. Believe it was from David Simon's The Corner but an early scene was New Year's Eve and as the hour approached everyone started taking cover before people started shooting up the sky and a hail of lead came down.

When Your Job Sucks

Suggestion from someone who hasn't published squat:

I was thinking of a LaFond guide for the general tourist to Baltimore. Of course, most will stay in the general confines of the Inner Harbor area but there are probably heads up areas within and around that area for which you could provide practical advice ("this bus stop has a high concentration of transvestite muggers and this bar is best avoided after 9", etc. & etc.). Last time I was up there I was on edge when going to the local 7/11 right next to all the hotels as there were just kids hanging out inside the store but peering out the windows, just keeping the whole block under observation. WTF? Were they that bored or was my inner alarm right that they were up to no good? Cover stuff like that for the out of town dumbass that is in town for whatever reason.

As I was kicking that thought around in my head I think you could easily produce your own HarmCity version of Broke-Ass Stuart's Guide to Living Cheaply in San Francisco. You're style, in a way, is similar. Stuart just doesn't list cheap and good places to eat, interesting stores, and things to avoid and look out for in each neighborhood but also usually provides funny personal anecdotes concerning about the bars he lists. You could probably do the same thing for Baltimore and take it in the direction you want to but could be a bit of a practical guide and humorous or dramatic anecdotes.

Thanks again for the writing.

Scott

Scott, thanks for the suggestion about the guide. As my search for Crazy Mark has been fruitless, and people like the write-ups I did on the bars my first night out looking, I think I should continue that. Right off the bat I can warn readers, that if you come to Baltimore, don't go looking for Edgar Alan Poe's grave at dusk—seriously. I'll stick to bars, cheap eateries, skanky joints, and places tourists need to be wary of. I will start this column in two weeks. In the mean time, if anyone has an idea for a title, please place it as a comment below.

How about The Poor Tour?

If it sucks just say so.

As for your question about recreational gunplay on the 4th, yes, yesterday, beginning about 9 p.m. the two bruthas in the rental two doors to my right begin firing their guns, a 9 mm and a 20 gauge. Then the home boy that lives behind me one street over got out his 38 special and popped that off. As far as I know no one was hit

That 7-11 you went to was the **very first business to get looted during the riots!** Kids between 13-16 take work as lookouts and runners for certain persecuted entrepreneurs along Howard, Liberty, Charles and Light, on the grid where Baltimore, Lombard and Pratt cross these streets.

When you are headed back into town let me know what areas you want info on.

The Poor Tour
WTF? Addendum : Building A Harm City Book with Reader Input

© 2015 James LaFond

Just saw your WTF post about my suggestion.

There's a couple of 7-11's nearby but if we are talking about the one on Mercer Street getting hit first then the riots were right there in the tourist zone. Cops abandoned that area?

The reason why the world needs your guide: I went to visit Poe's grave but it was a Sunday morning. What do all the Medical and Law students do? I think I saw some residences by there but they must batten down the hatches at night and only come out in the day!

When Your Job Sucks

Thing is I went to Baltimore to see a show at the Hippodrome Theater, right next door to the grave, the night before and just went there mission minded like you write about; being aware and a fast pace down W. Baltimore St, there and back. Is the drama by Poe's grave at night predatory, meaning thugs come there to purposefully hunt soft targets like tourists and students or is it just spill over from nearby neighborhoods and that's where they are hanging out and it is a tense time for locals and students alike?

Finally, the area you described the kids are keeping under observation for entrepreneurs is right there in the tourist zone and business district. Another WTF? Who are they selling to? I'm guessing many of the middle class tourists or "straight" office workers are customers, i.e. the same people that are also afraid and complaining about the kids and crime.

Please don't feel obligated to answer my questions directly as it could be some good topics for your upcoming series.

My final unsolicited suggestion: I do think that The Poor Tour or whatever it will be called would make for a good stand alone book, a la' Stuart, and I'll buy the MF as soon as it comes out but hope that the book would contain information not already published on your web page.

-Scott

Scott, I am going to take all of your suggestions and answer all of your questions, except one. The entire book will be published for free, one chapter at a time, on this site. This has become part of my editorial process. What will not go up for free are the photos of the locations.

I shall call the book The Poor Tour.

It will be dedicated to Scott C., as you have inspired it, and when complete, I'll send you your complimentary copy.

The Poor Tour shall be photographed and published by Mescaline Franklin, gonzo publisher of Forever Autumn Press, and urban blight tourist, from the rival urban canker sore of Camden New Jersey, who has expressed a vague interest in publishing such a book, as he too went looking for Poe's grave.

As for the Hippodrome Theatre, back in the early 1980s, a former boss of mine, named Glen, saw a movie there. He then went to his parked car and realized it was blocked by a line of men filing down an alley. They told him that they were standing in line to receive a $50 blow job from Puerto Rican porn starlet Vanessa Del Rio, who was waiting at the end of the narrow alley. So, Glen said, as related to me, "What the fuck. I've got fifty, I'm in! And you know what, I think I was number fifty! There was like twenty guys behind me. She was seated on a milk crate between two uniformed cops. I'm really not sure if it was her, but whoever it was she could have sucked the chrome off of a trailer hitch, so it was fifty well spent!"

As you can see, Scott, cops do have a history of protecting illustrious visitors to our great city!I just thought you would appreciate having been so close to such rich Harm City history!

Fortunately for you and others the local victims of white oppression do not know who Edgar Alan Poe was, and that stoned white dudes have been dying of exposure in Baltimore for far longer than they realize.

What do our out of town university students do that live in such areas as Charles Village, Govans, Gwynn Oak, Canton, etc.?

Why they sometimes are raped and killed like a young lady in Charles Village, or beaten into a coma like a graduate student in East Baltimore. Mostly, they play FBI

100,000 Wildebeest Roulette. Basically, stupid white people survive black predation the same way that stupid herbivores survive lion predation, by flooding the hunting matrix and emerging as one of the 90,000 out of 100,000 college students who are not mugged, beaten, raped or killed in Harm City!

As for your 7-11, it was the Howard Street one that got hit. The one you went to, in the same tourist zone, did not, as far as I know. I can tell you that there was no police protection in the tourist zone, and that bouncers and doormen and ball park ushers did most of the security work. A friend of mine's wife was beaten into a coma within sight of police lines and they did not even try and retrieve her body. The hub of tourist activity in Baltimore is the corner of Light and Pratt Streets next to the Baltimore Convention Center, across from the Leg Mason Building, and in sight of the Falon Federal Building and the waters of the Baltimore Harbor. That is where this middle aged lady was dragged from her car and beaten by black men, and where I documented numerous incidents in When You're Food. It is the place where I encountered **The Seven Dwarves Of Pratt Street**.

The Baltimore Police Department does provide tourist security for some events, like the Tall Ships Celebration, but not for others, like Saint Patrick's Day. It takes planning to pull off that kind of security, and since the only people planning during the riots where the gangsters and hoodrats the tourist zone was overrun, as depicted by my interview with Boomy the Hero Cabbie in War Drums.

The drug customers in the tourist zone are often not tourists. The way Baltimore is laid out most of the bus lines cross at the Inner Harbor or within three blocks. The #64 bus from Anne Arundel County, south of the city, intersects with the #19 bus that comes from near the Baltimore County Detention Center and Courthouse to the north of the city. The #64 dead ends at North Avenue! Look, never get caught on North

Avenue, and avoid bus lines that end in the ghetto. These bus lines intersect at Light and Pratt. These two lines constitute a wholesale drug pipeline, with the #19 passing the two major Baltimore City Court Houses and Detention Centers, where many of these deals are arranged.

Thank you, Scott, for the inspiration to do some location based writing. As the project moves forward, you, or any other readers, may feel free to suggest a location that should be investigated with an eye toward affordable survival, for the tourist, student, or visitor to Harm City who is not content with playing FBI 100,000 Wildebeest Roulette. If you are soon scheduled to visit our wonderful town, give me the date of your arrival so that I can make sure my post precedes it. I'd hate to have you reading about not—never, ever—heading West on North Avenue just as The Sand Town Crew begins to swarm over the hood of your rental car.

Harm City Pigpen
Police add insult to injury after mugging, By Connor Meek

© 2015 James LaFond

Adam Swinder was beginning to doubt my indictment of the BPD and checked the Harm City Letter of Record and forwarded a link to the story at the bottom of this page.

The hipster bicyclist that wrote this letter to the Sun Paper is astonishingly clueless, which leads me to believe that he perhaps immigrated from Planet Manpurse. I can't salute that gang of kids enough for placing this guilt ridden liberal at the bottom left of the food chain where he deserves to be feasted upon.

Imagine, if you will, the arrogance, of some lone, unarmed, sissy, riding a bike in a wood, near dusk, in a city renown for black on white violence, in close proximity to a black ghetto, whose youth have used this very park to practice firing their new guns, jump in recruits, murder snitches, plan attacks on police officers—and have gang bangs?

When Your Job Sucks

While we wrap our heads around 14 year old gang bangers gang banging, let us also wrap our heads around the fact that this is no longer 1903, and Teddy Roosevelt is not going to send the marines to punish every band of colored persons who dare to a lay rude hands on a member of the Master Race. Conner, that only works when European armies are wiping out colored people on a bloody regular! You would have been safer in Angola in 1976.

Thank you, sir, for emboldening another dozen or so black youths, who might now make the mistake of trying to take something from me, which might just put me behind bars for the rest of my life. Please, instead of encouraging black on white crime, ride that bike across the Jones Falls Expressway at 8:15 a.m. this coming Monday morning!

Better yet, preserve yourself for the zombie apocalypse—which I hear is nigh—so that I might stake you out for the zeeks!

Okay hipster immigrants, how about if you at least watch The Wire before moving to the town its black residents refer to as Bodymore Murderland.

Thanks, Adam.

http://www.baltimoresun.com/news/opinion/oped/bs-ed-city-police-20150705-story.html

Murphy's Govans Bar
A Poor Tour Backstory from JimBob BroHeem

© 2015 James LaFond

JimBob and I now have a regular weekly discussion on my bus home and his to work. yesterday he asked me, "Well any ideas on new books?"

"Yeah, One of my readers suggested a poor tour, a survey of the bars to go to and not to go too—eateries as well."

"Christ Bro, that will be an encyclopedia—and you'll probably get killed somewhere along the line—which would go along ways towards insuring flush royalty checks for your inheritors... Listen, I worked in over a dozen bars and have drunk in over a hundred since the eighties. I can give you some leads to look into—that bar that was low end back in the day and maybe still opened today—places with character! Unless of course the yuppies have gentrified them."

"Please tell me you're not going to the block house on Sinclair Lane."

"The Cedonia Inn—have to, a point of honor."

"Fuck that! Take a rifle company at least—you know Enfield's, pith helmets, get yourself a navy thirty-six in a shoulder slung holster and prepare to duck spears!"

JimBob's voice was echoing deeply through the confines of the ebony humanity packed bus.

"I'm going to check it out with my new publisher, Mescaline Franklin, a white kid from Camden New Jersey."

"Well, have fun with you masochistic friend, and don't forget to duck. My favorite in Fells Point was 'The Bar' just the fucking bar. Has a sign out front that says bar— still there. Place was dirty as shit—filthy, no amenities, no food, us wait staff from the restaurant trade we loved to get together there en drink after eleven."

The ten year old black kid seated next to JimBob is perking up, perhaps at the mention of his ancestors somehow throwing spears at the white bearded man across the aisle with the note pad and pen, listening to this odd ramble of the ancient white ape, regarding him like some relic out of an ancient world of high adventure.

"Jerry's Belvedere over in Govans* is a reliable dive. Old man bit it a few years back but his sons are still managing to attain the same low quality service their old man was renown for. The place should be a gold mine, but they barely get by."

"The real dive was Murphy's Govans Bar. Just down the street from the Senator you should get two food rushes, one per a show. If you have a good kitchen you make bank. Cheap beer and you keep the college kids coming. The owner—Murphy—was a stone cold alcoholic—a total drunk. He drank the profits. Couldn't pay for trash pick ups, so emptied the dumpster with his car and dumped the trash in someone else's dumpster. He would sublet this kitchen to this dubious character who used to bring whores into the kitchen and fuck them—right there on the prep table—while he was cooking. Let's just say I suspected his sanitation. A little afternoon delight—fucking the whore—and then back to flip the burger! What's not to like—need anything extra on that, pal?"

The young boy is looking up at JimBob with big eyes, like a priest who just found out that God farts.

"Now, I drank there because I worked down the street and the beers were cheap—the draft. Of course, you needed two coasters for every draft, one to put the beer on so that the sweat would not liquefy the dirt on the unclean bar top and have mud dripping down your wrist, and the other to cover your beer in between swigs so that the roaches falling out of the ceiling did not end up doing the backstroke in your beer. Old Murphy never had money for an exterminator."

*York Road and Belvedere, just below where Northern Parkway crosses York, above the Senator Theater.

The Hamden Grill
A Poor Tour Back Story from JimBob BroHeem

© 2015 James LaFond

All the while, between each line of his monologue on the ideal drinking establishment, JimBob BroHeem had a rapt audience, in the form of a wide-eyed black boy of perhaps 11, who had the window half of the seat occupied by JimBob, as we spoke to each other across the aisle.

"Now Hamden, I lived there for a while in the late eighties—worked a couple of bars, drank them all. Learned the three beer rule; that I'm an asshole after three beers and have to move to the next bar, because I'm going to get kicked out in any case. Never been into the violence aspect of bar life. So my favorite place was the Hamden Grill; a good place to land when the violence was becoming inevitable.

"So you have your stupid white men getting off work with their pay check. No brothers allowed—not back then. A paycheck and an idiot—soon to be a drunken idiot. The perfect date. The purpose of the bar is to separate the one from the other. Rather than make that the job of the bar maid or bar back the poker machine does the trick. There was this one dude who would put his entire paycheck into the poker machine. Once, after he did that, and began drinking his last beer, an old man sat down at the poker machine and hit! The guy got up and charged at the old man—charging around the bar. I didn't say anything, just headed to the Hamden Grill as the night wore on and the friction between the small minds and increasingly empty pockets caused things to heat up.

"The Hamden Grill, oasis of madness. This was the set up:

"No furniture; a veritable arsenal waiting to happen at great expense, none—you get tired, go the fuck home.

"No tap, because that requires a walk in cooler—fuck that, too expensive.

"No bottled beer, because those are weapons.

"Just coolers packed with cans and top-loaded with ice as you pull the cans out of the bottom. All they needed was an ice machine, and they had that figured out, low maintenance.

"No dart board—missile weapons, could even take out the barkeep.

"No pool tables—hence no deadly cue balls or clubbed pool cues.

"And, with none of that shit, no reason to hire a bouncer!

"That's my kind of drinking experience, come on in, get fucked up, and get the fuck out."

JimBob's pint-sized audience, hands braced wide behind him so that he could peer up at the lecturer without turning his head, looked up at his craggy visage with the batting eyes of one who has discovered a lost world and is simply attempting to catalogue the wonders—Marco Polo like—as the strange white man who used the folded and dog eared newspaper like a mnemonic aide to jar his rusty foghorn voice with a tap to his forehead, rambled on about yet another dive bar lost to inebriated posterity...

What Not to Say in A Black Bar
Stoner Hippie Tony O in the Hood: A Poor Tour Back Story

© 2015 James LaFond

This is an old story from the early 1980s that I summarized in my first book.

My roommate, Ronbone, 6'6" 350 pound stoner hippie, went out to smoke magic mushrooms in the 'pine needle jungle' with Tony O, a 5' 10" 200 lb stoner hippie who wore 'coke bottle' glasses.

After Roonbone missed their exit, and the next one, and the next one... They ended up in West Baltimore. Wanting to have something to drink while they drove all the way back around the Baltimore Beltway, they stopped at an Edmonson Village bar. Tony O said, "I'll be right back with a six pack."

Sometime later Tony O had yet to return to the car. Getting worried, Ronbone entered the bar and saw Tony O's mop of hair in the hand of a large black man who was pounding Tony O's face into the bar top. Ronbone waited politely for the man's arm to tire, and then motioned to the man indicating that he wanted to remove Tony O, who was now slumped over the bar bleeding. He grabbed his body and his glasses and took him back to the car.

It has been over 10 years since Ronbone died, and I can neither recall if he got a six pack or call to ask him about it.

I do recall what he told me about the conversation with Tony O in the car, as this entire story was built around telling me what an unreasonable asshole Tony O was.

As they drove off Ronbone asked, "What the hell did you do?"

Tony O responded, "Well I walked in there and the bar tender is ignoring me and all of these niggers are giving me the evil eye. I was pissed. Finally I say, 'Hey, what nigger do I have to blow in here to get served?'"

Ronbone, forever impatient with stupidity, said, "You mean you couldn't think of anything better to say than that?"

Tony O was indignant, "Oh, I see, so it's my fault—blame the victim!"

They managed to stop in Highlandtown and get a six pack of Mickey's Malt Liquor and made their way home, drinking and driving through the back streets of East Baltimore.

Garnished with Dead Hoodrat Annually
Jimmy's Famous Seafood & Clementines

"Dude-

"I'm a bit of a chef and a total food junkie. No I'm not fat or overweight. Just watched a clip on great restaurants serving famous Baltimore food and want to know if you've been to or know of these restaurants on your turf.

"- Jimmy's Famous Seafood (CrabCakes and Crab Sandwiches)

"- Clementines (Bacon wrapped meatloaf)

"My mouth is watering! Spare no details."

-Ben Rumson

I can no longer afford to eat at either of these locations. I did go to Jimmy's three times when I was making good money, and am treated to a meal at Clementines occasionally by my more successful son.

Jimmy's Famous Seafood is a well-regarded restaurant by seafood lovers of my parent's generation. Younger people have not taken to it as the food is on the bland side. Crab sandwiches are just plain disgusting. An entire soft-shelled crab, caught after shedding his shell, is eaten as a sandwich filler whole, eyes, guts, shit and all. I have never eaten one, anywhere. My mother assures me that Jimmy's crab cakes, which I have never cared for enough to pay the steep prices, even when I had the cash, are among the area's best. Honestly, the supermarket I work at sells store made crab cakes for $5 and they are as good as anything I've had out.

When Your Job Sucks

The service ay Jimmy's Parkville location is excellent. The service at their old Dundalk location, just inside the city near the old GM plant, was horrible when I went there in 2009, with one half done appetizer taking 45 minutes to arrive at the table. My son and I walked out in disgust and grabbed a cheap burger. We were the only patrons in the joint at the time, at 4 in the afternoon.

Clementines is only a half mile from where I sit. A dead hoodrat was served up fresh this time last year right at their front door—killed by a .25 auto, I think. The owner of this joint is singlehandedly keeping the urban blight at bay by hiring a neighborhood janitor, and getting special police units walking a beat. He also owns the Green Onion snob grocery on the corner of Hamilton and Harford, thirty feet from where the White Vice Lords stabbed a predatory panhandler for beating up a crippled panhandler and taking his spot.

The atmosphere is excellent, with a mix of old furniture, couches to lounge on and books to read. This store front was once a furniture store where I bought the furnishing for my mistaken investment in Baltimore housing back in 1982. There is a small bar with microbrews on tap and imports in bottles, and a wine selection that my son actually approves of. The service is excellent and the portions are small. However, the quality is stellar. The best time to eat at Clementines is for breakfast.

The chef makes his own sausage, bacon and meatloaf, with sausage and cured meats hanging in a plexiglass walk in for the diners to see. The meatloaf dinner is too expensive for me. The only dinner I can afford is soft tacos. However, their ala carte breakfast selection is really the best example of lean cured meat I have eaten, and is not any more expensive than going to Denny's. The meals are served with artisan bread and the restrooms are actually clean. Items that appeal to working class and lower class blacks are not placed on the menu. So the only clientele you get here is the hipster crowd, which means really nice polite black families, and a bunch of sissy white people who will not speak to anyone that they did not arrive with.

The Crack Head Meter
How To Tell When a Person is Drug Addict, When You Pass On the Street

© 2015 James LaFond

I have been using this test since cigarettes went over five dollars a pack. The dynamic is, that since a rock of crack or a hit of heroin each run $10, and that a drug addict devotes his life to scrounging for that figure, any purchase over $5 is totally beyond the dope fiend pale. Lowlifes have always used cigarettes, usually a request for a free one or a light, as a means of getting close to someone they may want to shakedown, rob, or attack.

Ever since the price of smokes in Maryland has topped $5, begging for cigarettes has doubled. But, the big thing was that people began asking to buy a single cigarette for a quarter, and then for 50 cents, as they simply lacked the discipline to save up more than $5 and not bypass tobacco for better dope, resulting in their $5.40 to $7 pack of smokes costing $10.

When Your Job Sucks

In Baltimore and Central Maryland most crackheads and heroin addicts also smoke cigarettes, and usually not as regularly as an ordinary smoker, until they have kicked the hard dope and go full bore three packs a day into the tobacco. Currently, my neighborhood is host to about two dozen heroin addicts, who are the privileged children of successful white flight settlers who own homes in Harford County, and are about my age. These barely privileged kids do not have the funds to be dope fiends the suburbs, so they are pioneering in groups homes dedicated to drug use, resettling the areas their parents fled from. In my area all of these types play the single cigarette game.

As for the black community, you will note that almost every unattached adult male wants to buy cigarettes, an indication that vast numbers of urban black men are crack and heroin users.

My best guess is that if you assume that the person trying to buy a smoke is a crack head or dope fiend, then you will be correct three out of four times.

Cowbell Put My Head in the Noose
An Accidental Experiment in Inebriated Anthropology

© 2015 James LaFond

Below is the most I was able to manage inscribing as to my plight after coming home from the mixed-race sports bar, which was not very mixed last night, barring this cracker's presence, that is.

I just got in my front door at 12:35 a.m., I'm alive, I'm drunk, and I'll tell you about it when I wake up, hopefully without a hangover that is as good as this...

On the desk in front of me are two pens, a coaster with hand written print on both sides, a cell phone—outdated—a wallet with two business cards full of notes and Bernie's phone number, a bank receipt from—yesterday I guess—documenting my brokedness, and nine one-fucking dollar bills—and I'm still running!

See you in the morning!

Now that I am awake and enjoying a hangover that feels about as good as my last concussion, I shall attempt to make some sense.

Last night at nine, or so I had been informed by Dory, it was Hawk's party. Of the 40 regulars, half white, half black, he is the most liked person. Among the older black men he generally sits as the chairman during the various inquests. Dory told me, "Oh Baby, he loves you—you have to come. Of all his white people you are his favorite."

Yesterday evening was going surprisingly well, writing wise. There was also the specter of my laxity where covering the neighborhood crime goes. As I wrote yesterday afternoon I heard the police chopper three times in search patterns and listened to seven different police cars fly past my front door. And I am far behind on my poor tour entries. I laid down for a nap as I did not want to brave the night after having been up for 21 hours without a rest. After sleeping from 7 to 8, I threw on a very ragged outfit, including torn jeans and my 30 year old "please dad" bomber jacket. I was armed with three pens, and placed Hawk's gift in my pocket.

When Your Job Sucks

As I walked down White Avenue I noticed there was less foot traffic than normal.

When I got to Harford Road I noticed that road traffic was low, very low, and that the only apparent activity was at the pizzeria and the gas station on the left, and the bar farther down the street to the right.

I crossed the street above the ATM machine where various packs of teens skulk waiting for victims to ambush back in the neighborhood. As I crossed the side street where two cretins named Skidmark and Cumstain once tried to sick a pit bull on me, I looked straight ahead and saw that three dark hooded forms where standing back among the shadows of the church. These boys were about 15-16 I noticed, and unrecognizable to me as I neared them. This made them the fifth trio of boys [six if you want to count Skidmark, Cumstain and their dog named Yo] to set up at this darkened corner under the broad reaching oak tree in the shadow of the church. I was looking at then narrowly from under the rim of my hat, and did not make eye-contact, but looked ahead and began to pass them.

The leader, a middleweight, spoke, "Hey Mister, would you like to party?"

Still stepping I looked up and noticed that he was stepping away from the light heavyweight and the welterweight. All three had hooded black sweatshirts on and had hands in their pockets.

"Come on back here," he beckoned, with a nod to the darkened grassy court under the tree and beside the church stairs. His two friends began spreading out, hands still in hoody pockets.

I looked him in the eye and his face pinched up and flushed as his head jutted forward under his hood and he walked toward me, to late to cut me off from passing on the sidewalk if that is his intention, saying menacingly, "You disrespecting us?"

I made sure I had a pen in each of my pocketed hands and declined to maintain eye contact and walked on by. This brought him down on the sidewalk behind me with a declaration, "Go on you bitch-ass Nazi. We'll get you later!"

When Your Job Sucks

My mission was to say hello to Hawk, wish him happy birthday, and give him his signed copy of The First Boxers.

At 8:30 on a Saturday there are usually 5-10 whites and 20 blacks. There were 10 whites, including three members of two mated homosexual pairs. There were hawk appreciation banners, two tables of food, and seventy of hawk's black friends. And people kept coming in.

The average age of the men was sixty. The average age of the women was 40. the men are all retired or employed and most have a history of college sports participation. Dory now assured me that this was not a birthday party, but just a "Hawk is Cool" party. I was wondering about the three young thugs and about the opportunity to study what appeared to be an entirely different culture than what they represent. I really did not feel up to dealing with those three and decided on staying until ten instead of leaving right away. The entire staff was working, all white except for Cowbell, **'Cowbell's Broke-Ass Odyssey'** who was doing his janitorial duty in white suit, fedora, and snakeskin shoes.

Russ and Nancy bought me a pitcher of beer and we talked about the event, and who was who. I managed to slide around through the crowd back to the corner where hawk habitually sits, past Black Superman, into a group of older fellows who recognize me. haw is speaking with two guys in their forties. This is obviously a patronage network. Based on the coaching jerseys worn by the various younger men, and the level of fitness among the older fellows, I observe that this is a black version of my Uncle Fred's extended network of athletes and coaches which functions still for these men fifty years removed from their days playing college ball. The difference with this group is that the men over 65 are not former athletes, but their uncles, mostly former military men.

Hawk stopped his conversation an introduced me to the two younger black guys who were not pleased to see me at all. I gave him the book and he told them about my couching and writing, and said that the only objection he had about my Greatest Boxer book was that, "Ali didn't even make it into his top ten!"

When Your Job Sucks

I was greeted with scowls by all but the eighty year old man in the pimp outfit who winked and declared, "'Cause Ali was a dancin' bitch. Joe Louis was the man!"

The younger fellows were now more comfortable in their kneejerk hatred for me so I rubbed it in. "I put Ali in the fifteen slot, I think, maybe lower, which has certainly earned me a berth in various hells."

I hugged Hawk, promised to stay a while, and returned to my seat by the front doors.

Eventually, I found myself sitting between two young women as the last of the whites were walked out by Annie's son. I am not counting Big Jim, the "Yeti" who feasted greedily in all nine fried chicken platters even as he mumbled about "blacks taking over." Russ informed me that the giant hillbilly was angry over having both of his eyes blackened in an encounter with a recently arrived group of young thugs. The beat cop was no longer patrolling Hamilton for reasons unknown, and this autumn was turning out to be a mugging season.

Finally, at 11, Annie's son asked me if I would leave now so that he could make sure I got home okay. He told me that it was basically last call for white egress in force. I declined, said good night as we shook hands, and then decided to continue my interview with Cowbell, wanting an update on his fate. I asked him where he was staying and if he was okay.

He looked at my ratty threads and said, "I'm at a nice spot, way out the Ten line at Security [where the Social Security Administration is located]. There still eight beds if you need one. You lookin' harried brutha. Need a number?"

"No man, I'm returning a room just up the street."

"Oh, I tried dat shit, en got sick a havin' ta fight fo my life every night!"

Such conversations were mere punctuations for the experience, which for me, was one of people watching. This was a karaoke party. When white guys do this it is a chance to laugh at them. hawk and four of these guys sounded as good as the recording artists, and even dud duets, continuing after the music was done and still managing to make it sound like a song. One of the white barmaids sang two country songs, which people listened to, though they had a hard time continuing their dancing. Another barmaid sang something that my untrained ears slotted as opera, but who knows. An older white guy was playing pool with three of the older black guys and a young dyke in the back.

The dapper Puerto Rican who supplies the karaoke machine was their in his suit observing the five men and twenty women who were dancing along the long side of the bar. I now, after two pitchers of beer, had adopted the strategy of outwaiting the punks by the church, and needed to use the bathroom. this was a harrowing experience as my narrow ass darted between these dark dancing bodies who seemed to be wanting to use me as a pinball in there living dance machine. When I got to the "stage" and went to dart around hawk, who was dancing and singing, he reached for me and said, "No you don't, Jimmy—you dancin'"

An ancient pimp hand belonging to this man **'Gonna Throw This Drink Back'** patted me on the back with approval as I managed to evade Hawk's clothesline attempt and made it to the men's room, where the Puerto Rican dude was critiquing the accommodations and making estimates on his smart phone as to how many more customers he could attract to an event if the men's room was more spacious. Then I had to do it all over again.

I was now thoroughly entrenched as the non-dancing white mascot in 30 year old surplus threads among the well-dressed patrons, while people just glanced occasionally at Big Jim the Yeti as he feasted like fearful children looking at a cigar store Indian.

Then came disaster.

The three sisters, and the other six sistas who had been line dancing between me and the radiator and ATM machine, were running out of men. One of these women was a particularly aggressive dancer both athletic and over endowed, sweating profusely. As the call went up for "more men" to dance with, Cowbell entered the fray and comported himself like a hero, virtually clearing the floor of women still wanting to dance, until it was just him and the sweaty dynamo of a vixen. Finally, even Cowbell, after virtually having clothed sex with this woman in front of a hundred people as the Yeti ate more fried chicken, reeled away, wiped his sweating forehead with his fedora, and patted me on the back. "There you go Brutha—she's all yours. Got her worked up for you."

As I looked at him dumbfounded—and kind of hurt, really—I was seized by two gorilla strong arms and whirled out onto the ancient unfinished hardwood floor. It occurred to me, as I was spinning around and being bounced from breast to hip and then spun around again, that this woman was a whole lot stronger than I. I heard Hawk roaring with laughter somewhere behind me—not altogether sure were behind was and certain only that my orientation would forever change rapidly as this women manhandled me. Cowbell was grinning with unconcealed glee as the song ended, the woman threw her arms up around my shoulders and dragged me over to my stool where she said, with vivacious sincerity, "Glory be, finally, a white man for me!"

Cowbell slapped me on the back and said, "'That's all you Brutha—Cowbell be lookin' out!"

She then put her foot up on my foot, pinning it to the rail, sat her meaty hip on my thigh, and manually hoisted one massive breast up with both hands and dropped it on my forearm. I'd say it weighted ten pounds.

I had to leave, to make my escape.

I said, "I have to—"and she cut me off, "No you don't" Don't leave."

I spied the back door open, to the parking lot and the church lot where the three thugs had earlier skulked. Checking my wallet for a remaining capital bill—and there was one. I placed it on the bar in front of her, bought her a Jim Beam and Cola, and said, "If you an me are hooking up I have to say goodnight to Hawk."

She beamed bright brown eyes up at me, smiled, and let me slip out from under her, backing up so that I could not get out the front.

I made my way to Hawk, where he was dancing with Dory, and said, "Man, I got to go!"

He said, "You sure, Bother, in the night? It's getting bad out there again. Stay and I'll give you a lift."

I then pointed to my "date" with my chin and said, "I'm more afraid of what's in here—I'm over and out."

I ran—yes, ran—out the back door, past the dumpster, around the razor wire fence, and then slowed as I neared the grassy church courtyard, pulling out both pens from my jacket and running lightly up the stairs behind where the thugs had been waiting in their ambush position, to find out that they were thankfully gone.

The walk home was nice, without a soul on the street.

I got home, still wondering how those people in the bar came from the same seed as the three thugs staking out the ATM and the churchyard, certain only that they will be replaced by three new models within the year.

It's time to go clean the mats, train and coach.

"Once Upon a Time"
Philly Mo and My Favorite Cop Story

© 2015 James LaFond

I know a half dozen dudes who have been arrested for pissing on walls and sidewalks in Baltimore. It's a bad idea. Most cities have ordinances against urinating in public. So, when you are out on your version of the poor tour, be certain to relieve yourself at the urinal before you head out for that long walk back to your cheaply parked car...

Mo was in town for work this week and we had a few beers together last night. The following is a recollection from the 1970s he related in his muted style.

"If you are familiar with the elevated subways of Chicago, we have the same thing in Philly. I grew up in a poor white neighborhood. You ought to look up Police Commissioner, and later Mayor, Rizzo, a real character, came to a riot wearing a cummerbund ready to kick butt.

"Once I was heading down the staircase from the elevated train and there was this other young man relieving himself, leaving a puddle of stuff there for commuters to deal with. A police officer caught him, and gave him a speech on how it was wrong to leave this puddle for other commuters and made him take off his shirt and mop it up. Then, he informed the young man that it was against the law to ride the subway without a shirt on and directed him to be properly dressed when he boarded the train, standing and watching with an approving eye as the citizen pulled the soaked shirt back on his person."

Now that is a cop I approve of.

A Moment at a Ghetto Eatery
A Poor Tour Cameo

The Chinese woman spoke some English as she took my pork fried rice order and fixed it, barking in unintelligible gutturals to the older man preparing another dish for the fat, bearded, thirty-something white guy next to me, who kept looking at me nervously.

The black chick with the big ass was not nervous, so I decided to spread the love and ogle her hind parts as I leaned on the counter and nodded to the Chinese woman as she asked, "You want duck sauce? You want soy sauce? You want mustard?"

The black girl was un-phased and batted her fake eyelashes above a reluctantly crooked smile.

The white guy was more nervous than before. So, despising weak white men, I slid a menu out from underneath his six-pack that he had set on the counter without excusing myself. Once he swallowed hard I was done being a jerk, for the day, and was thrilled, while testing the twin pack of chopsticks against my palm to see if they would be any good as a shank, to find the following imprinted there.

Welcome to Chinese Restaurant

please try your Nice Chinese Food With Chopsticks

the traditional typical of Chinese glorious history

and cultural.

A $7 meal for two and a disposable shank—though you have to choke up on it, stabilize it with thumb and forefinger in a saber grip, and hit something soft.

Macho Nachos
Your Low Budget Wingman

Are you an urban dude expecting a visit from a suburban babe?

Is this babe likely to return—or course she is, as soon as you train the bitch out of her!

Then, offer to cook. Say, "Baby, I've got dinner on the stove—just come straight over. I don't want you spending time or money feeding me. I just want you."

Of course that's complete bullshit, other than the fact that your cluttered microwave top can be loosely defined as a stove top.

When she arrives, put on the meal, a plate of nachos. Babes love nachos. Even bitches love nachos.

Use the authentic border jumper favorite, Charras sea salt and Chile Limon flavored tortillas, bought in the ethnic food aisle frequented by Latino construction workers.

Cover liberally with what ever kind of cheese Mister Mike has marked down for being close dated down at the ghetto grocery. Feta cheese is best, as chicks like it but will be so salty with these chips that they will be nigh unconsumable by a woman, especially one worried about retaining fluid!

She will eat enough to get thirsty but still be hungry.

Trust me, I tried this recently and it has the two desired effects.

First she will get really thirsty and with you having nothing to drink but beer, emotional lubrication and a resignation as to her purpose will soon overcome her.

Secondly, this babe will never again show up at your door without a home-cooked meal!

You are set, bro. One box of condoms [$4.99] and a bag of chips [$3.19] for under 10 dollars should net you three dedicated cooks for as long as you can juggle them.

Oh, and don't forget your ownership manual:

Bro, buy this book and it's only a matter of time before the bitch queens that have ruined your life will have their hairstyle altered to accommodate your beer coaster!

Taking Back the Night
Bringing in the Four-Wheel Cavalry

© 2016 James LaFond

Yesterday Mescaline Franklin and I went out on the Poor Tour, to two suburban bars tucked away at the end of two dying streets, beneath a railroad track. The bars will remain unnamed and are fifty feet apart. Two years ago the larger bar was frequented by a mixed-race crowd and there were numerous stabbings, two related shootings nearby, a parking lot rape and an exodus of the law abiding clientele.

As we walked up to the front of the larger bar an angry, middle-aged, black man was outside and needed an ear to gripe into. He was so angry that he had a hard time gathering his cigarette to place between his two missing teeth on the top front left of his mouth. Noticing the pristine state of the rest of his dentition, I decided that he was long in the habit of speaking angrily.

He said, "A nosey muthafuca piss me off. A nosey muthafuca always pluck my nerve. They ain't nothin' good 'bout a nosey muthafuca. A nosey muthafuca gonna git you killed. Nosey muthafuca eyeballin' me, in my bidness, askin' me where I from! I hates me a nosey muthafuca!"

I said, "Are you coming in for a drink?"

For answer he gave a grumble and lit up as we entered to see about a half dozen middle-aged mechanics, two older men, and two young tattooed rednecks. A hag, a hard woman, a slut, and a barmaid, who looked like she could have been the plaything of a blind mobster, rounded out the denizens.

We had a nice stay at both places and I took note of the measures taken to make certain that blacks do not want to spend time there.

1. Available music is limited to rock, metal and country

2. There is no beer on tap

3. Miller beer is not sold

4. Malt liquor is not sold

5. Iced drinks are not sold—you drink your liquor straight. Blacks even ice their beer. Not having ice is a huge affront to a black bar patron.

6. The bar that had beer on tap only had Bud and Coors light, no regional cut-rate beer like National Bohemian.

7. There are signs posted that no foul language will be tolerated, which excludes virtually all African American dialogue.

8. The bar with tap beer opens early and closes early: 9 a.m.-10 p.m.

9. The bar that stays open late is owned by a woman who employs a Latino manger, so that no white employee will have to command blacks to leave for cussing or violence and bring a discrimination charge. Besides, Blacks tend to a virulent hatred of Latinos, as demonstrated by the man outside.

10. The TV programming in the large, late bar is set for law enforcement reality shows, baseball and racing.

When Your Job Sucks

When Your Job Sucks
Brant, Biff and Beyond

Twenty years ago I got bumped. The chain I had hired on with lost the lease on a store, so I was bumped by a senior union employee. This man could not do my job, but was entitled to my hours. It was bad enough that I had taken a 10k pay cut to get out of management and just work. But now I was losing 5k more and would have to freight this 60,000k a week dairy case just the same, as the guy that bumped me ate doughnuts and stared at the ceiling. The chain would be opening another store within six months. I just had to tough it out.

The wife was not happy.

Working the dairy aisle made life complicated. Every employee used this aisle to access the stockroom, the break room, the entrance. The store was laid out to force the customer through the entire thing like a maze, and it worked. We had almost hit a million dollars grand opening week, and I had gained survival points—and had saved my job—by actually refilling the case in one night. When the cuts and bumps came, the manager asked HR for permission to "hide" me as he would need two men to replace me. After years in lower management and all of that stress, stocking freight was like a sport to me, therapeutic. So for me, the price of job security—mere high production—was low.

The L-shaped dairy aisle was also used by the vendors: the bread, snack, soda, frozen pizza and ice cream suppliers that sent in their own people to deliver and stock their goods. All of these guys were now struggling to keep up with their route once being handed this monster store, only the fourth of its kind at the time. Venders typically top out in retail on the hourly scale, and after declining to get into management buy a route, and kind of work for themselves. These guys would compliment me on my work. Then, one day, two vendors were walking down the aisle arguing over who would get received first. They come in first with their ordering machine, then go back to the truck, pack their order, and then line up to get checked in by the receiver.

This was Brant, the PepsiCo Vendor, and Biff, the Imperial Ice Cream vender. Brant, a 40 year old former high school sports hero with an arrogant personality and mafia style voice, was denigrating Biff's route, his working ability, that he sucked, that ice cream sucked, that his regional company sucked, etc. Biff was a smooth talking 24 year old pretty boy, far less aggressive, but smarter than, Brant.

Biff stopped behind me and pointed to the wall of decked freight I was working through, about 4 feet high and 72 feet long, all going in the case before it got warm. Biff was inspired, "Well Mister Tough Guy PepsiCo, I will be getting salesman of the year, because I'm hiring my man here as a merchandizer, fifty dollars a day and all the ice cream you can carry for your rug rats. How about it pal."

I shook his hand on that and he said, "I know you can get all this shit done by eight—not like these grocery retards in aisle eleven [as he looked at a man who owed him money on a football bet]."

"I'll be ready," I said.

Biff slicked back his hair and sneered at Brant as he taunted, "Yeah, Tough Guy. You're looking at salesman of the year. They'll be dicing your route up and I'll be partying with the honchos!"

Brant went right for me, "Look Mo, you're a man, not a sissy like this here fast talker. Work with me and I'll pay you forty for only two hours work, rather than get stuck on this slow-ass motherfucker's truck until seven at night while he's chasing skirts on the front end [register chicks]. You wanna work with me!" he said, as he punched himself in the chest.

I said, "Hey guys, I'm a whore and there's enough to go around."

I worked out a schedule that had me getting off at eight, working with Brant for two hours, and then hopping onto Biff's truck at ten and working with him all day. I also picked up a job with Pizza John, and a job at two independent markets that were on Biff's and Brant's routes. I was only home from 7 to 9 p.m. for the next year as I worked these six jobs. In many ways I lived a lifetime in that year. During this year I was a fixture in 34 stores, dealing with thieves and bums on the back dock, rival vendors, the nuts working inside the stores, and my crazy employers who were both paying me cash and taking me along on their trucks against company policy. Brant was in numerous altercations over dock access and Biff needed help because he spent 2 hours a day on pay phones placing bets with his bookie and had a girlfriend in half the stores he served. The best looking female store employees typically date and marry vendors.

When Your Job Sucks will tell the stories of on the job craziness with Biff and Brant, and also other fellows who I have worked with in supermarkets. The stories are all about working thankless jobs, and in many cases are the job loss stories told to me by coworkers, such as truck drivers, when they told me why they suddenly found themselves working in a food store in the middle of the night at age 40.

The stories will include:

I Wanna Happy Meal!

The Pitcher's Mound

Tony O

Mole The Man

Smoking Mike's VCR

Diamond Jim

Mama San

Brant's Jacket

Our Fag and Your Fag

Falling in Love with Sheep

Messing with Mister Glass

The Leg Breakers

Trash Man Sam

Big Tom

When Your Job Sucks

Sex on Wheels

In the Headlights

Get On In Rambo

Bowling for Bums

Wrecking Biff's Truck

Chaos and Control Mo!

Bonehead

Getting Mugged in Your Truck

Sanka en Buttafingas

"CCKKK—bitch!"

Twenty Cars Gone

Nasty Nick

'Shorty, Short'
A White Wednesday/Ghetto Grocer Reality Check

We lowly supermarket clerks have long resigned ourselves to being cussed at, demeaned, threatened, and even attacked—for rarely does a clerk go through their career without a customer striking, or in the case of women, molesting them. But sometimes—and this is not often—a thing happens which stretches the mental template of humanity to the breaking point.

The basic rule is:

1. Most black women are rude.

2. About a third of black men are rude.

3. Most food stampers are stupid, which really makes diplomacy difficult.

4. The only food stampers who are not rude are white men. Blacks and white women with food stamps are always rude.

5. The only non-law enforcement customers that threaten to harm employees are old white guys who want sexual favors from young female employees and black food stampers. I have no recollection of a cash paying black customer threatening me or my staff unless he was a cop, and I had two of those, a city cop and a transit cop.

6. The only white men who have threatened male employees are cops. I can name five white cops that threatened me or my staff, not as part of their job, but in seeking privileged treatment. I have also been 'flexed on' and glared at by two white cops while on the job in my present location.

What this points to is the aristocratic impulse to do violence to those who serve you, which seems to arise exclusively in police of both races, women of both races, and black men who do not work. Working black men and mature black criminals flush with cash are generally the most polite and civil customers you will deal with. Once when barring entrance through the exit door after hours on Christmas Eve, I had a black cop threaten to "beat you wherever I see you" for not letting him shop after hours. Another black cop on another occasion did the same. Ten minute later a young black criminal with his homeboys came up to me with a knot roll of bills and offered me $1,400 to bring him a gallon of milk, so that his baby's mother would not be mad at him for staying too late at the bar and missing the supermarket. When I declined, he was polite and understanding and wished me a merry Christmas. I can only imagine what a bitch she was!

When I used to manage a store and hire people I had one introductory speech for all customer service people. "Look, every type of person on earth, with the exception of third would dictators and certain types of serial killers, shop in supermarkets. You will get it all. So be prepared and don't take it personal."

What is more and more obvious to me as real wages shrink, and adjusted wages whither for grocery clerks, and welfare benefits increase, is that we are the mud-tilling peasants of the Welfare State. The welfare people, and the scumbags who buy as much as one third of all food stamps at 50 cents on the dollar from state subsidized drug addicts, are the lords on their mighty steeds. Indeed, the most common vehicle driven by welfare recipients is a late model SUV. A few weeks ago a $700 food stamp order was packed into a shimmering white Escalade at my local market.

And now, since the riots and purge, police are no longer responding, or are electing to wait an hour to respond, to calls for help at supermarkets in the city or the county. As I entered work on Monday night at midnight I did not see Alf the pimp and his two white whores sitting in front of the dollar store. I also did not see Rico Suave and Trash Mouth, who have been causing trouble lately. The store was doing a brisk business as food stampers, and those who buy discount food stamps, bought sodas and snacks by the cart load.

I spent an hour in the stockroom and cooler sorting my dairy order, then worked up a cart of yogurt, which took me to about 1:30. I made a hot chocolate at the coffee pot and walked up front to pay for it and get a shopping cart for my cardboard. There was a nine-year-old girl shopping, with a cart and open wallet, seeming very studious about her business. She was a short half-black half-white mix with her hair straightened, in the way that Ajay assured me costs hundreds of dollars a month to maintain.

When I checked out Bubba, who deals with all of the scum, not just the ones buying whipped topping to snort the gas, looks at me with heavy lids hanging low over his 21-year-old eyes and says, "I hate people, I really do."

I went out front and noticed two 13-year-old wanna be thugs loitering by the door. To my right was a woman who resembled the child so much that I was relieved that she was not shopping parentless. The woman had a baby carriage which she was pushing in small circles on the sidewalk. She too had an expensive hair do.

An hour later I come up front to have lunch and find out there has been a commotion I did not here from my refrigerated habitat. I ended up interviewing the parties involved.

Shorty Short in the Market

The nine-year-old girl essentially shopped solo as her 25-year-old mother tried to follow her around the store, but was, according to Steevo, "Either stoned, or fucking retarded—real, shit your stupid pants, retarded."

During the course of her jaunt she came around the corner of Aisle 11 as Steevo pulled down his stair stepper off the over head and rammed him in the back with the cart at high speed as she screamed "like a fuckin' animal, man."

Steevo stepped back in amazement and let her go by.

She then approached Jack and snarled, "Your fucking store sucks, bitch!"

Jack admitted to "a what-the-fuck moment" as he got out of the little demon's way. This kid has already figured out that she is the tyrant of a parentless world in which the law—if ever applied—tends to favor the most savage and violent child over a well-meaning adult.

The girl brought a series of order to the register and, one-by-one argued with Bubba over the total. If a particular selection did not seem to be worth, let's say 10.14—which was the total of one of the orders—she would scatter the goods across the belt and then go and shop for another order. Her remarks to Bubba were more along the lines of him being stupid and incompetent for not correctly tallying the orders, rather than profane. She did say, "This store really sucks! I like the other store!"

Bubba said, "Then why don't you shop at the other store?"

The little lady responded, "Fuck you. Where are the cookies?"

As she went off to buy cookies, as the candy she had selected was too expensive, her mother mumbled in response to Bubba's questioning look, "I'm really tired of her."

Note that the woman was wheeling a silent baby around the entire time.

Finally one of the orders was tallied to this non-counting designer-attired waif's approval and she made the transaction with cash.

Bubba said, "I was totally shocked that it wasn't a food stamp order."

Shorty Short then demanded, "Call us a cab."

Bubba, peering five feet down from his great height, asked, "You want me to call a cab for you and your mother."

"That's what I said! Can't you hear?"

Bubba picked up the phone and made the call. When he asked the young beast what her address was she darted over and ripped the phone out of his hand as he looked on in amazement, and began calling the cab dispatcher a "stupid white bitch" for not knowing where she lived. She then unleashed a stream of profanity replete with F-words and hung up on the dispatcher.

Bubba called back and apologized to the dispatcher, and managed to get the address from the mother. Eventually the cab arrived and carted off this load of obnoxious fury, who, shall come to maturity in world that owes her everything, shoulder to shoulder with legions of other privileged children of the Welfare State, as working people work for ever less serving their savage needs.

I Wanna Happy Meal!
When Your Job Sucks #1

© 2015 James LaFond

I was working with Biff on his ice cream truck, which would be my home for 12 hours twice a week after I got off work, helped Brant with his snack route, and began working with Biff when both vendors stopped at the same small independent market. Tuesday and Friday, when he put in his big orders, were usually the days I worked. As we got to a location Biff would often slip away to the pay phone to call in his bets to his bookie, or to the front end to chat with a cashier.

At this particular private supermarket, where the ice cream section was right up front by the registers, there was not much point in the latter. On my first day on the job with him he scanned the front end for potable babes and saw… old women.

"Good God, Jimmy, would you look at this wasteland? This is a travesty. This is what you get with independents. The wife of the owner makes sure there's no hot babes to distract the old man—dude this is awful! Now Mars, they have their act together. A bunch of Italian guys run that outfit. Just wait. Half the front end is hot, and the chain of command is structured by looks: good looking register babe, really good looking front end supervisor, and smoking hot office manager."

Biff, all of 22 years, would go on and on at every stop, and while driving between stops, as to the quality of the women out and about, or at the next stop. He was proud to have wrecked his truck three times looking at babes. But on this first stop at Big G's Market his musings as to the quality of customer service that results from sexist hiring practices were soon quieted by a ruckus not ten feet away at Register #3.

A nice looking lady in her mid twenties was shopping for her family, with her four-year-old boy standing in the cart and a wedding band on her finger. The boy was holding onto the cart top and demanding, "Mommy I wanna happy meal!"

She kept shushing him, with some embarrassment, as the customers to right and left, and the one behind, considered her disobedient child with raised eyebrows or smiles, depending on their nature.

Biff was paying extra attention to this customer as she was the only attractive woman in the store. He was winking at me and nodding, which was his way of saying, "I'd ask her out if she wasn't married *and* had a kid."

Finally Mommy had had enough and patted the little beastie on the butt with her fingers and hissed, "We are not getting another happy meal today!"

Then the little brat pulled the pin on the nuclear family grenade and said, "Mommy, if I don't get a happy meal I'm gonna tell Daddy about you kissing Uncle Joe's peepee in the basement!"

Silence descended on the front end of Big G's Food Market like an invisible curtain. The kid, noticing with an elated raising of both eyebrows what an effect his declaration had had, what power he had just wielded, grinned and, straining onto tippy toe, began to repeat himself, only to have his mother cover his mouth and cup the back of his head and gasp, "We will get a happy meal!"

The woman was mortified as the customers and employees stared. Finally her cashier began ringing again and the other register lanes resumed scanning and bagging, though with customers glancing sidelong at the blushing woman. She might have been horrified, and the customers and staff shocked, but the boy and Biff were elated. Biff turned to me and whispered, "Oh Mommy is a little freak—Biff-Biff's got the radar out!"

As the woman left with her smiling son rocking joyously along in the cart next to the grocery bags, and Biff strained on tip toe to get a parting glance at her silhouette [she was wearing a white sleeveless blouse and lime green shorts, and seemed athletic, but petite], I said, "Do you think the kid is going to work that for a large milkshake?"

Biff blurted, "Shit that kid's face is going to be on a milk carton if he doesn't watch out!"

Woodstock and I
A Reader Submitted Story for When Your Job Sucks!

We were doing work orders, Woodstock and I.

We received a call about a possible irrigation leak on a home.

We pulled up to the address and Woodstock said, "Shit I was just here last week. The bitch inside is crazy. You're coming in with me."

The irrigation access was a crawl space in the woman's bedroom closet. We lifted the plywood lid, crawled in and began to look for the leak. Finding no problem, we were in the process of climbing out with Woodstock in the lead, He put his hand on the wood ladder and turned so fast I thought he had injured himself. He grabbed me a pulled me back and said, "Oh fuck!"

I replied, "What the hell?"

He motioned me to the ladder and said, "Look up."

Being a dumbass I walked over to the opening of the crawl space and looked up. Imagine looking into the eye of an 80-year-old old shaved beaver. The woman was standing over the opening in a skirt with no panties.

Woodstock said, "I told you that bitch was crazy. I'm never doing another work order at this address until we hear of her death. They don't pay me enough for this shit."

That beaver burned a hole right out the back of my head. I replied, "Me too."

That is something you never forget, unfortunately.

Emanuel

The America that Liberals Want
Shorty Short, Her Retarded Methadone Addict Mother, Five Thugs and the County Pork

Last night I arrived at work at five minutes two midnight, and noticed that Office Manfriendly—the bald prick that harassed me in 2011 **Officer ManFriendly**—and a pretty blonde lady cop were interviewing witnesses amidst trash strewn at parcel pickup.

Five thugs leaned on the entrance and mumbled threats at the cops, including this one that I heard from a half-Mexican half-black thug with dreadlocks, "If dey gonna arrest anybody up in hea' dey gonna be a purge up in dis bitch."

I shouldered my way through these punks, who I was certain I could crush in a fight, and they spread as easily as black pussy on Saturday night.

I walked by Bubba to clock in and he grinned, "Shorty Short was in here raising hell—God I hate people!"

'Shorty, Short'

I spoke to the night captain and found out that the trash was from Shorty Short throwing the trash bins over the railing after he made her leave. She also destroyed two shopping carts*, tearing the wheels off of one and snapping off the welds with chimpanzee quality retard strength as she rampaged across the front walk calling clerks, customers, thugs and cops "Motherfuckers and bitches."

*I examined the carts and found that the welds were snapped. I have done this when breaking down old carts for scrap salvage, and I required my gloved hands and work boots to snap the welds.

She had been cussing out and assaulting employees using the handicapped scooter cart as a ram while her stoned mother followed listlessly behind on foot, nodding out and drooling.

Crazy stuff like this happens at the end of a long month when the dopefiends and their children have been weeks without food money on their orange card. Giving children and drug addicts thousands of dollars at one time and expecting them to make it last for a month is one of Liberalism's best ideas yet.

The police refused to arrest the mother or the child. They knew the pair from the hospital where the one pig does outreach work. The pigs wrote a note to the social services counselor, itemizing all of the misbehavior, and handed the note to the mother, who is virtually the terrorized slave of this maniacal child.

The night captain said to me, his eyes wet with unshed tears, "I really do think these people need help. And they are just being referred to the very people who have not been helping them. That woman is not just stoned. She is mentally handicapped. What is a matter with this country? This is not the country I was born and raised in—it's like some sick animated movie!"

I responded, "There is a third person we are not seeing—a father probably. Somebody got that retarded mother hooked on drugs, and she learned the sex, violence and profanity from somebody other than her zombie mother."

He shook his head in abject sadness and mumbled, "I tell my father this stuff and he says I need to move to South Carolina with him—that every city is getting like this."

I was thrilled, personally, to come face to face with another sign of the End Times, when everything falls apart and I might get the opportunity to defend myself against my attackers, my hunters, without fear of the hated pigs taking me down.

I walked by Steevo, who Shorty Short previously rammed with a shopping cart, and he shook his head darkly and snarled, "They ought to have their pussies cut out. I'm sick of these welfare bitches running our lives. This has got to stop."

I counseled, "Don't complain too loudly. The people we work for pay big lobbying bucks to make sure welfare stays as it is, large lump sums of money for unspecified purchases in the hands of those least able to wisely mange it. As a retailer, we benefit from the impulsive dollar. Supermarkets in upscale neighborhoods are run on skeleton crews because those people make smart purchasing decisions and there is nothing left for payroll."

He groused back, "You ought to go cheer Zach up. He's having a bad day—was on the bus stop with that bitch."

"That bitch," who we nicknamed Shorty Short, is a mixed race female who leads her twenty-something mother around like the Princess of some bizarre kingdom followed by a weeping lackey. She is just over four feet tall and weighs perhaps 70 pounds. We have guessed her age as anywhere between 9 and 12. She has not even begun puberty, has not a bud on her, not a curve to her sluttily attired body. The mixed-race group of thugs who had been supporting her against the cops—who she also cussed out and threw stuff at—ranged in age from 12-40 and was of a more politically correct three-race mixture in various phases of miscegenation.

I got my pad and pen out for Zach, who was depressed and tearful, feeling like he was all of a sudden the citizen of a pointlessly sick world.

"Dude, I was on the bus stop with those two for thirty-five minutes. She was dancing, stripping and offering her body. She said to every one of us men there stuff like, 'Wanna put some dick in this ass? Wanna bust a nut in this ass. Do you like drunk bitches? I'll get drunk for you. I'll suck your dicks like they've never been sucked!'

"—I don't want to repeat it anymore man, it's making me sick."

"Seriously man, it ruined my week. This was down in my neighborhood on the other end of the line [Dundalk Center]. You know I want to get married, have kids—but how, in a world like this? To make things worse, when this older lady began to scold her and she froze up for a second, this black dude took her side. I suppose he's a customer. And there was this white dude there with his daughter, and he let her hang with this girl and his daughter was imitating her!"

I left Zach alone as he was truly upset.

Readers, I give you the future Queen of America, a bi-racial hellion violently acting out with the support of menacing black men, under the noses of limp-wristed police and with the blessings of Liberal social services employees. The Liberal attack on the American family has finally born its rancid fruit. By the time Shorty Short is 13 she will be pregnant. At 20 she will have five children, receive $2,500 dollars a month in cash and food stamps, and live in a suburban townhome for $100 per month.

The best part about this utopia is the karmic aspect. Just as all of those disgusting Liberal Baby Boomers—who have turned the greatest nation in history into an overwhelmed mental health ward—are confined to scooter chairs, our most recent generation of hyper-violent, legally immune and comprehensively entitled youth will be thoroughly conditioned to prey upon the remnants of our Worst Generation.

May these fiends feast on the wrinkled remains of the Woodstock Degeneration.

'Don't Make Me Chase You'
White Wednesday at Hoodrats R' Us

© 2015 James LaFond

It is the end of a long month and retail food has become a war zone. So many stories from fellow ghetto grocers have been coming in to me by phone that I can only offer a sampling. Just keep in mind, that if welfare payments are ever halted for more than a day or two, that any American city which does not receive free money will erupt in riots and looting. The monthly nature of the welfare distributions are such that the ghettos are on the verge of rioting after the 27th day of any month, and that every additional day that month lingers the more heated the situation becomes. Note that the Baltimore riots were timed for the end of the month, a gang strategy that police have still not picked up on and will likely never recognize for what it is, as their welfare comes weekly or bi-weekly depending on the jurisdiction. This month is particularly bad because July money came out early at the end of June because of the 4th of July. [The reasoning for this escapes me even though my boss explained it clearly enough.]

I just got a call from Roger, the manager of a ghetto food store, the only white man on the scene. Last night his book keepers, two black girls, were walking round the side of the building to a bus stop when they ran into a man standing outside of his makeshift tent in the bushes, peeing. They all three screamed and the girls ran back inside. TeeTee, the more aggressive girl, grabbed a produce knife and went back after the squatter, who surrendered, pleaded for mercy for the homeless, and assured her that she had frightened him as much as he had her.

Mall security will now be escorting these helpless females to the bus stop.

Just before Roger called me, a known shoplifter, who is usually good for hauling $200 of merchandise at a time, came through the front door with his pregnant wife. A female customer came to Roger and said, "I just saw that man beating that pregnant woman and telling her she had to come in here and steal or else he'd whoop her some more."

Roger notified the uniformed police officer on duty, spoke to the man who was shoving merchandise in his pants, and then gave chase as the man fled out the door.

As Roger ran past the pregnant wife she threw herself on the floor and began crying, "Amblance—amblance!"

Roger tackled the shoplifter on the parking lot and dragging him back in as the woman pleaded that she was going to sue because he had trampled her, although a dozen people saw otherwise and the cop assured her that her lie would be exposed on the security video.

As Roger handed the man off to the cop the woman began to leave, afraid now that she would be arrested for the stolen goods she had on her. Roger said sternly to her, "Don't make me chase you."

The fetus-infected woman ran. Roger caught her easily without taking her to the pavement, and brought her back to await the ambulance and paddy wagon with her husband. They were both hauled off to Central Booking this morning.

Roger was beside himself with dismay over the acceptance of theft at his new store. "You just would not believe how brazenly people steal here, and how acceptable it is to most of the customers. It's like working in some zoo for the mentally retarded and insane."

A Question of Customer Service
When Your Job Sucks #2 : Biff on the Chopping Block!

© 2015 James LaFond

Biff, the Imperial Ice Cream route driver who I helped twice a week with his extensive route, had two slow days, when he hit all of the 7-11s and farm stores. Seven sleeves of ice cream was regarded as the minimum for a second stop for these once weekly accounts. Since they primarily sold high-priced Ben & Jerry's, that was still worth the time and gas. Imperial Ice Cream did take pride in good customer service, and would make one stop to spruce up the ice cream display even if no purchase was needed.

Almost immediately, after going to work for Biff, I found out he had one out of the way 7-11 that he stopped at twice a week, only bringing in three sleeves with each visit. The reason for this was that the woman that worked during the day had sex with him in the walk in behind the milk racks. He even recounted one harrowing tryst when they heard the door bell ring and she left him standing there with his pants around his ankles staring at the crates of milk in the 38 degree dairy box while she rang out a customer. He said that she always admonished him to remain in this attitude while she took care of "interruptions," and that she always returned to "finish what she had started."

Then one day, a few weeks later, Biff was a nervous wreck. It turned out that he had bragged to a fellow route driver, who coveted his oversized route, and who had ratted him out in hopes of getting him fired. Biff was beside himself with worry: he was buying a house and a car, was engaged, and was $6,000 into his bookie and losing money every week. His supervisor and the regional manager were going to the 7-11 in question to interview the owner about Biff!

I didn't know what to say.

At the end of the day we shook hands and he said, "Well Jimmy Jam, if I still have a job on Tuesday I'll pick you up at eight. If I buy the farm this is it."

I told him something about pleading good customer service, and hoping the cashier would not rat him out.

He gave me some extra Ben & Jerry's ice cream for the family and tipped me $10, making it a $50 day.

The following Tuesday he picked me up wearing a shit-eating grin. I cannot remember his words. His narration of the events though, that terminated in that wry smile, remain clear.

The route supervisor and regional manager had called ahead to the owner, and arranged to meet her at the store, at the time that Biff would typically show up for his first stop of the week.

When they arrived at the store they noticed an attractive woman operating the register and waited for her to finish serving her customers before asking to speak with the owner. The woman then indicated that she was the owner—or co-owner, rather. Her husband worked the overnight shift and she worked the day shift.

The regional manger asked if they would be able to speak with the clerk that normally checked in Biff's order about his customer service. She informed them that it was she who was the clerk on duty when Biff delivered his ice cream; that his customer service was "excellent" and that she must insist on a third order every week!

The lady insisted that "Biff Biff" was "needed" at least three times a week!

Biff triumphantly grinned and began singing the song "I'm just a gigolo!" and continued to belt out the tune all day long, any time the spirit moved him to sing his anthem along to whatever other song happened to be playing on the radio.

Biff had gone from jerk to god in the eyes of management, who gave him a pat on the back and directed him to continue providing exceptional customer service at the stop he now called "Seven-I'm in Heaven."

'Seven-fifty a Pop'
Seven Greedy Dwarves Building the America Liberals Want

Joel works at one of Maryland's largest wholesaling facilities—a huge warehousing and distribution operation. When I saw him this Saturday and asked him what the latest adventures were at work he seemed kind of pinched in the face about it. Knowing Joel, I figured it had something to do with the Spanish and ebonics speakers who are shipped in to work as temps. It has been irritating him that at 45 he has to learn a new language in order to communicate with employees who often end up being fired for stealing. I have graciously promised to serve as his ebonics coach, but can't help him a lick with the Spanish.

Joel then went on to say, "Over the past few weeks employees on the night shift have been having their cars vandalized. The vandals are taking the air bags. They get seven-fifty a pop for airbags. Well, it turns out that it was seven employees from the day shift that were coming out at night and breaking into cars and taking the airbags. Security apprehended them."

Not wanting to upset Joel, I compassionately asked him, "How many white women did they arrest for breaking into those cars?"

"None," he grimaced.

"So this was seven white dudes that did all of this breaking and entering."

He looked at me darkly, not answering, so I continued to forge on as a responsible member of the Press Corp should, "Would these thieves happen to be victims of your white oppression?"

Joel snarled, "Jesus, Jimmy, they were temps. Don't get me all riled up. It's enough to drive a man to drink."

Last year over 60 employees were fired for taking a part in an organized theft ring at Joel's place of employment. It makes no sense to Joel that his employer continues to replace thieving employees with new employees from the same demographic.

Old Cleve
When Your Job Sucks and Your Coworker is Great

I was a ranch hand as a young man, changing sprinkling pipe, mending fences, hauling hay, moving cattle to new pastures. I used to work with an old gentleman. He had a drinking problem but still managed to work hard. I loved to hang around this old guy just to listen to his stories. We were watering grain which sounds simple but is a very hard job, they flood irrigate grain which is like walking in a rice paddy, just less water. Your wear rubber knee boots in 90 degree weather. The soil is clay mixed with organic material from the alluvial deposits of the last ice age. It sucks you down, like stepping in thick molasses, very good exercise for your calf and thigh muscles. Cleve would bring water and beer in an ice cold cooler. He would let me have a few beers when we were thirsty. I really enjoyed this despite the hard labor.

When Your Job Sucks

There was an old orchard next to one of the grain fields. We would sit under the apple trees and drink beer at noon. He would tell me stories about life in the valley in the 1920s. It was like a little piece of heaven to me. Despite his drinking problems I was amazed how hard he could work at his age. I would guess he was in his late 50s in 1970. He worked like this after I graduated high school in 1975. When I came home to visit my parents in 1982 I was working out in the West Desert of Utah at a beryllium mill.

My dad said they had found Cleve dead on a tractor, he had been brushing the meadows that spring for the new growth soon to arrive, he had a massive heart attack and died, but was still sitting in the seat slumped over the tractor having run into a shallow ditch, killing the motor. The first thing I thought about was sitting in the apple orchard with him drinking beer, and smiling knowing he died at his post still working at his old age. Hope I receive the same providence from nature as he some day.

Ishmael

Swamped in Satan's Wake
As Baltimore Area Wal-Marts Close at Midnight a Local Grocer is Overrun by Foodstamp Freaks

© 2015 James LaFond

In retail food Wal-Mart is 'The Great Stan' 'The 800 pound Gorilla in the room.' However they achieve this on a slim profit margin, only made possible by low payroll and high volume. I'm currently out of the grocery loop, with my head buried deep up my allegorical canal trying to locate my metaphor.

Why Wal-Marts in the Baltimore area now closed after midnight is not known to me. But I have a hunch it has to do with loss prevention, or rather the lack of it. Most likely one store detective is trying to cover two to three stores, relying on middle-aged female managers and overweight female security guards to stop the near looting proportions of shoplifting.

With the example of overnight Wal-Mart customers we had last night, I can only imagine what a nightmare it is to be a midnight shift manager in one of those heinous temples to low quality excess. The one local cop who cares about overnight employees stopped in to warn us about the horde approaching, as there was also a teen event letting out at midnight.

-There was the 350 pound bald woman with the two 450 pound bald teenage sons jiggling on by, in three varieties, one black trio, and two white. I have come to the conclusion that viewing pro wrestling causes premature baldness.

-There were a half dozen 50-60 year old fat men with canes cruising around on handicapped carts.

-There was the sixty-year old hippie woman in the denim tent-like skirt who came to stand next to me as I kneeled stocking the sour cream. Let me tell you, her cream was a great deal more sour than mine. The funk rising from her heavy skirt rivaled the dumpster behind Al's Seafood.

-As a half naked couple walked in wearing mere threads, skipping down the aisle in dirty bare feet, the girl's belly button tattooed around in the form of a vagina, Bubba the cashier groaned, "I so hate people. This night is going to get even worse."

-No fewer than six women and five men lined up with great anticipation to use our very small single stall restrooms, as if crapping in a public place was some sanctifying rite of—yes, I'm going there—passage. I was breaking down freight in the cramped stockroom next to the woman's room and felt like a sewage worker. These chicks did not even bother closing the door, but left it wide open—I think the cows broke the door spring.

-Two wannabe gang bangers showed up with their shirts draped over their necks, showing off the unreadable tattoos on their tootsie roll torsos.

-A third of the customers were eating and shopping at the same time, tossing their empty bottles, boxes, and crab cake trays, pistachio shells and shrimp exoskeletons onto the shelving.

-One 40-year-old couple argued over the brand of hotdogs they would purchase as her body odor wafted up from exposed armpits, as she was dressed like Daisy

Duke, with a physique closer to Laurence Fishburne than his daughter.

-At about 1 a.m. a family of giant man-babies and sagging mammas miscalculated their order by a large sum. Steevo was assigned to "re-shop" the merchandize, and stopped by my work station to gripe,

"Must everything these lazy fuckers by be shitty? They can't buy soap to wash their ass but they can eat more in a month than I eat all year—and they just have to come and shit in our restrooms. Let me ask you this, if they know they have a certain amount on their card, how come they can't add that shit up as they shop?"

"That is the appeal of the ten for ten sales, and for that matter dollars stores, Bro," I sagely answered. "But still, even shopping three at a time they can only count up to thirty—then you're into multiplication. That's like asking me to build a space ship by six a.m."

Steevo was now casting disparaging glances down the aisle at a gay couple. The flamer was a muscular black male of 20, who wore tight designer torn jeans and a plush white shirt knotted just above his nipples. Steeve groused under his breath, "The fuckin' zombie apocalypse needs to hit—real zombies, the kind that will eat these fuckers!"

He groaned softly and hung his head as the male slut began skipping toward us. He then replaced the pudding packs that the welfare people who could not count would have to live without as I stocked the French onion dip, and got back to the original topic, "Dude, seriously, how hard can simple addition be?"

The flaming gay man-doll of glistening ebony skipped by Steevo in a slow sashaying way and lisped, "One plus one equal two. Two plus one equal three, three plus one equal four... "

Steevo's eyes bugged out of his head as he snarked, "I feel much better knowing that that faggot can count how many dicks go up his ass! The way he swings that thing he probably knows his multiplication tables too."

The most interesting customers of the night were handled by Tia, my personal wallet-blocker, who protects this author from the nefarious wiles of sluts of all describe. That story will be told as an installment of Your Trojan Whorse. Look out for Tia and the Ho-Train.

Operating a Hoodrat Trading Post
The Pitfalls of Selling To and Employing the Sainted Oppressed

© 2015 James LaFond

Recently the small grocery store where I work has been overrun with midnight shoppers, such as tattooed drunk freaks with chin piercings shopping at 2 in the morning with a gaggle of toddlers. I recently surmised that this had something to do with inventory shortfalls at Wal-Mart causing that discount retailer to stop remaining open overnight. High theft might occur when one only has one cop playing video games on his smart phone and one zombie security person at the door to keep track of hundreds of employees and customers. In low pay work places employee theft can be expected to account for 60% of inventory loss.

I take the bus to work with five clerks who work overnight at the Golden Ring Wal-Mart, which is one of two Wal-Marts from which we have pulled additional afterhours customers.

I have gleaned the following information from two vendors who serve our store and the Golden Ring location, and two employees of that Wal-Mart. I recently visited the Carol Island Wal-Mart to familiarize myself with the entrance and exit scheme. These places are not easily policed due to the accessible layout, which I suppose hints at their rural origins. I could only imagine what a nightmare it would be trying to mange one of these things in Baltimore City, where 30% of the population believes it is their duty to steal, 30% believes it is their right, 30% believes in looking the other way, and only 10% understand that theft is eventually reflected in higher retail prices and lower customer service.

The Wal-Mart at Golden Ring, in the Rosedale section of Eastern Baltimore County, in 2014-15 reported the highest losses in the history of Wal-Mart, compared to stores nationally and internationally.

In 2015 losses are currently at 3 million.

In 2014 losses totaled 6 million!

I guarantee you that Wal-Mart loss prevention was working their asses off trying to stop this after 2014's record shortfall, and still, halfway through 2015 the thieves were on track to equal last year's theft projection.

To give you an idea of how desperate a retailer has to be to close overnight, the tiny supermarket where I work, which is about half the size of a Wal-Mart's food section, lost 1 million dollars per year when it closed down overnight in 2009.

The weakness of an operation like Wal-Mart is that with such a low gross margin, any one theft will nullify 10 sales.

Loss By Category

Electronics, 65%

Toys, 15 percent

Gun/ammo, 10% [This is such a good idea, to stockpile guns and ammo in a low security facility staffed, in part, by Baltimore City residents!]

Automotive, 5%

Other, 5%

Puerto Rican Strippers
An Epic Early 1980s When Your Job Sucks!

© 2015 James LaFond

In 1982 I was training new clerks for a supermarket night crew. The strange thing about this was that half of these guys were twice my age—some older. There were lifetime jailbirds, finally no longer dangerous in middle age. There were construction workers who had beaten up their boss. And there were truck drivers, who either had failing bladders or had eaten so much speed they couldn't sit still any more.

I figured Rudolph to be one of the latter. As we were working in the aisle, I asked him what most in his crestfallen position had offered, the reason for his settling for a $5 per hour job working harder than he had before, being bossed by some 19-year-old twerp.

He looked at me and Ian—the black ex-marine—and asked, "You guys promise not to laugh, right?"

Ian and I assured him that mirth was not on the menu and he told us his story, the words of which have fled my brain pan, but the plot of which is etched forever in my frontal lobe.

Rudolph had a drinking problem. One more DWI and he was out of a job. He drove a car carrier. He was taking a carrier loaded with cars [about 20, though I can't recall exactly], through New York and up into Connecticut. He had been given a sum of money that was adequate to lodge and feed him overnight in a comfortable suburban hotel.

However, Rudolph had one weakness beside alcohol, Puerto Rican girls!

Ian was in agreement that Rudolph was on his way to telling a grand tale of, well, the only thing that mattered to Ian—tail.

Rudolph could afford, with his motel fee, to buy a bottle of Bacardi, rent a room in a dive hotel in Spanish Harlem, and go to a strip club and procure high quality Puerto Rican companionship!

The man was a genius, Ian decaled, "workin' the Man fo all his ass is worth!"

I recall the funniest thing about this story, being that Ian, warned in advance that it was a tale of dire results which had deposited Rudolph right there onto that milk crate sorting canned goods next to Ian—just as his recent prison stay had deposited him on an identical pauper's stool—was following the story of Rudolph's Puerto Rican tryst with wide-eyed innocence, certain there was a good ending!

Rudolph, being so pained by his experience that he seemed to want to postpone the punch line as long as possible, assured Ian that the rum was oh so good, the babe oh so fine, the hotel not completely rat-infested…

Then, after some time, with Ian grinning big-toothed and wide-eyed on the milk crate next to him, Rudolph told of his waking up alone, his wallet gone, and running outside in a panic pulling on his shirt, only to stand in front of a car carrier that carried nothing but frames. Not a tire, not a moving part—not even the mufflers—of the 20 or so domestic sports cars [Mustang, Charger or Trans Am, I cannot recall] remained attached to the car skeletons.

Ian reacted as if punched, leaned back on his crate, and hit the floor.

I stood there dumfounded.

And so Rudolph became a grocery clerk at 40-and-change.

Urban Venom
Notes on How Entitlement Harms the Entitled

Last night I was eating pizza at a local pizzeria when a ghetto queen strode in to pick up her order. She had an expensive SUV on the lot and a pre-emasculated fatherless black teen standing in her ominous and expansive shadow.

The two girls working the counter were dolls, with a heavyset smiling white girl and a tall light skinned black girl being very helpful and efficient.

The mamma announced in loud aggressive tones that she wanted to speak to the manager, who stepped forward. This sniping at employees that are stuck behind a counter smacks of children thrusting sticks into the monkey cage at some sadistic zoo. As a retail food manager I was called about a dozen times a day to the courtesy desk to hear complaints about the lack of courteousness of the young lady that had been selected to work behind the courtesy counter for that very characteristic. These all came down to the customer having a bad day or wanting something for nothing, and was always aggravated by a sense of entitlement, either because the person was white and had worked all of his life and did not appreciate some 'young black bitch' standing up to him, was old and was retired and did not appreciate some 'young black girl' talking back to her, or was black and had been discriminated against all of her life, and did not appreciate some 'young skinny black bitch who think her shit don't stink disrespecting me!'

This incident was the latter, with a rhino of a charcoal beast homing in on some young slim red bone girl for not addressing her with enough respect over the phone. The fact was, that the girl's short tone was due to her extreme work load, taking orders by phone as she took orders face-to-face and rang out payment for already filled orders.

I wanted to say, "The girl was short because she was in a hurry to feed your fat ass," but let it go.

The woman held the entire pizzeria hostage with her sense of entitlement, pointing out over and over again that she was well-to-do, was a pharmacist, and singlehandedly kept this pizzeria in business—which some people might be inclined to believe on first sight.

Eventually, enough apologies voiced, the woman left in a huff.

When I left, I advanced to the two ladies behind the counter and said, "Excuse me, I'm in the mood to chew someone out. Which one of you girls is up next?"

Realizing that I must be an experienced retail person, they both smiled and pointed to the heavy set white girl, whose turn it was to take the brunt of the next irrational entitlement tirade, and chimed as one tormented customer service organism, "Me-Her!"

The immediate effect of this change of clientele as the area gets black, is that refills are no longer free at the soda machine, hours are increasingly limited, and there is no dining atmosphere available that does not challenge one's digestion. One of the reasons why blacks suffer so much from hypertension in urban environments is that there is literally no place to sit down and dine outside of a McDonalds. If this area continues to darken, the tables and chairs will eventually be moved, the counter will be caged in, fountain drinks will be removed, etc. The only place to eat will be at home, with no opportunity to relax in public, going out to forage, and then retreating to your lair with your food.

Lack of peace of mind, is not the only price paid by people who have been falsely educated by the liberal white media and academia to believe that they are objects of constant oppression and are due a fortune in compensation for the sins committed against long dead folks by other long dead folks.

I bought a bag of out of date marshmallows at work yesterday for 34 cents! Mush Mouth Mike, who works that aisle, forgot that many cases of these sweat treats were on his over head. Our boss, doing inventory, discovered them and marked them down from $1.19 to 3 for $1. Marshmallows just get stale when they get old and can be microwaved and used in hot cocoa. These taste fine. I would never sell out of date dairy, meat, deli, etc. But most dried grocery products are stamped with a best buy date, a pessimistic estimate of how quickly it will lose taste and nutrients, not an expiration date.

When I managed a city store, such a thing would have been unthinkable. Any product that was out of date that we might have tried to sell, was a sure sign to the oppressed customers that we were trying to get over on them. The health department would be called. Here are some examples from my personal experience.

I worked for Bel Garden in the 1980s. The old Polish couple that owned the store donated all damaged and out of date product to a Baltimore City soup kitchen. I was tasked with making sure this stuff was all good. I took this job seriously and threw out anything questionable.

One day, while I worked on the dented cans, tossing pin-holed and swelled cans aside, Miss Betty came to me and told me to toss it all, and forever, that a black homeless man got sick to the stomach after eating at the soup kitchen and there was an investigation that determined that the freshest possible foods had not been used by the soup kitchen. The investigation had implicated Miss Betty [an immigrant woman who had been born poor to a starving mother] as something of a criminal trying to poison the poor.

When I worked for Shoppers, B. Gaddy, famous soup kitchen queen of Baltimore, began sending trucks to pick up the massive stale overflow that all grocery store bakeries produce. Most grocery stores throw out 4 shopping cart loads of bread products and cakes per day. It was soon discovered that a starving black family had been poisoned by a moldy slice of bread, which was obviously a bio-terror attempt by the Jewish operators of the chain. Law suits came, and the trash chute overflowed once again and forever more.

Urban poor pay more for their food because their sons are entitled to rob the retailer, upping operations costs, their mothers are inclined to hassle the help, reducing employee efficiency and upping costs, and the legal profession is poised to sue any retailer who would dare offer food to the poor rather than money.

The urban poor—including retired white union employees and Korean War vets who I have often served—are infinitely poor in a deeper way. They are, according to our masters in politics and the legal profession, incapable and unfit to check a slice of bread for a spot of mold, or to squeeze the top of a can of beans to make certain it is not spoiled. Simply put, the modern urban poor are regarded as inferior to a baboon, a chimp, or a monkey, who all have the ability to check food for spoilage. Indeed, the urban poor are thought of as being as low as dogs or pigs, domesticated animals without the good sense to avoid eating rotten food.

This is an animal farm.

The Mac Daddy versus Big Shiv
Refereeing A Workplace Fight: A Vintage Harm City Repost

© 2015 James LaFond

I met the Mac Daddy in 1998, on the night crew of a Baltimore City supermarket. He stood 5' 11" and weighed about 340 lbs. There were a few things to admire about the Mac Daddy. First, he was a minor league linebacker, who was repeatedly ejected and eventually fined into retirement for excessive force when playing teams composed of off duty police officers. He admitted to being a dirty fighter who preferred the sucker punch. Lastly, he was a big black man who openly admitted to being under endowed! I comforted him with the factoid of Shaka Zulu's impotence, and he felt better.

The Mac Daddy talked like a pro wrestler, in the third person, and was generally known on the crew as Big Boy, so named by the 260 pound Silverback, whose real name was Israel Flood, an old school dude from the south who he fought to a draw in the lunch room. The Mac Daddy grew up in a tough area of Washington DC, and liked to intimidate "Baldamore bruthas" with his ominous street-cred. After Silverback retired, The Mac Daddy was the undisputed king of our domain—and I, his diabolical counselor—until Big Shiv came to work as our security guard.

Big Shiv was from Turner Station, a Black suburb of East Baltimore that dates to the pre-Civil War era. He stood 6' 5", weighed in around 450 lbs, and was a self-declared predatory homosexual. At 5' 8" 153, I found it quite troubling, to be standing at the urinal in the mens room when Big Shiv entered, as he was in the habit of whispering seductive threats into the ear of any man caught in this compromising position.

It was not long before The Mac Daddy and Big Shiv decided to fight for territorial dominance. As the resident expert on all things violent, I was approached to sanction their fight. Neither man wanted to be arrested or fired for slugging it out, so I was dragooned into service as the underground fight facilitator. Since we were working in a heavily policed up-scale White enclave, I strongly suggested they not fight outside. They also could not fight under the Orwellian gaze of the ubiquitous cameras manned by the Loss Prevention Department.

Fortunately for the recently un-punched man-cards of both of these notorious, but aging, thugs, I found a solution. Our milk cooler was 20' by 24' and had no camera within. I constructed a 16' square cage of parked pallets of crated gallon milk, which permitted each fighter his own private entrance from either side of the walk-in, which had two separate entrances.

The men would meet for battle in the middle of the ring and began fighting, according to no set of rules, on my call. I was only there to say "Go" and to witness the inevitable bad ending. As I hid behind a support beam like some early mammal observing T-Rex battling

Triceratops, Big Shiv landed a jab-straight combination to the formidable brow ridge of The Mac Daddy. Big Shiv winced in pain as his hands and wrists buckled on contact with the thick bony shield that was the forehead of The Mac Daddy.

The Mac Daddy was no technician, but he had good instincts. He left his head open and proceeded to punch the soft hands of Big Shiv with his own mutated paws, or as he referred to them "chump-hammas". Within two minutes Big Shiv tapped to fist punches, and retired with a bruised knuckle, sprained thumb, and sprained wrist.

Later that morning, Big Shiv asked me to walk up to the park with him so I could train him for the re-match. As we entered the park a yipping, five pound, white poodle broke from a bun-haired old woman and came prancing toward us. This thing was so small it could have lived inside of one of Big Shiv's size-17 boots, and rented space to local rodents. I was soon astonished to find Big Shiv literally climbing up my body; standing on my feet and getting as much as his body above my shoulders as he could. I thought I would snap in half at any moment. The old lady looked up in bewilderment, over my head, on top of which Big Shiv's arms were folded, as he pleaded down to her, "Is it a good dog!?! Is it a good dog!?!"

Needless to say I decided not to train Big Shiv, but I did make a habit out of interviewing The Mac Daddy at every opportunity.

'When I Was in High School'
When Your Job Sucks: Teen Jobs

© 2015 James LaFond

When I moved to Western Pennsylvania at age 13, the first thing I did was gravitate to the woods for my recreation. I soon discovered, in the streambeds, metal contraptions about the size of a child's shoe sole. I asked Mister McCaroll, the man next door, what they were, and he told me that some boy was probably trying to make money trapping muskrats and to leave them undisturbed. I eventually tried my hand at trapping muskrat and was a failure. I did manage to kill some rabbits with throwing sticks. But rabbit pelts only brought 15 cents at Pete's Surplus. I just let my dog tear them up. Interestingly enough, Ishmael, my host for next year's Liver-Eater Excursion, has offered to teach me the cruder points of ruining a creeping critter's day. As it turns out, Ishmael is one of those fellows who made some money trapping as a boy.

"When I was in high school, not wanting to get up at four a.m. to milk cows and then go to school, I trapped. I set traps for Mink, Bobcat, Muskrat and Beaver—I didn't even know what a cougar was yet, so don't go there. It was a way to get out of doors, out from underneath of The Thumb.

"In 1973 a Bobcat pelt was worth seventy-five dollars. A mink pelt brought ten dollars. Beaver brought fifty bucks. I only got three-seventy-five for a Muskrat pelt. I could skin a Muskrat in thirty seconds.

I caught six bobcats, fifteen mink, a dozen beaver and four-hundred-and-seventy-five muskrats. Milking cows, you received two dollars an hour. My investment for traps and pelt boards—some of which I made myself— was about a hundred-and-fifty dollars.

"I will show you how to trap when you arrive next fall."

-Ishmael

Ishmael, I'm particularly interested in learning how to set hoodrat snares—or would I use something bigger?—when we get together next year.

Tone
Work, the Best Medicine for Racial Hatred

© 2015 James LaFond

Tone was born and raised by caring parents in Baltimore City. Unfortunately he was a slow learner and was also black, which means that his peers would harass and alienate and attack any one of their number who made any effort to gain an education. For Tone, survival called, he cliqued up, and got passed through school barely able to read and not able to count reliably above ten.

However, even though he lacked the defiance to go against his peer-inflicted cultural conditioning and pursue an education, he also declined to get involved with crime. Tone was a decent, unremarkable, guy with a clear sense of right and wrong. Unlike many of his peers he had a father, who gave him that. Although Tone's ability to manage inventory was never going to be there, he did accept training and I was able to teach him how to build displays. His customer service was excellent and that counted for a lot.

Tone, like most of my black clerks who worked afternoons or overnight and had to travel through Baltimore on foot in the dark, was arrested on roughly a quarterly basis for being a black man on foot in Baltimore after dark. He was also attacked and beaten by innocent unarmed black youths on a few occasions. He would be out sooner rather than later, as he was not one of those knuckleheads that fought or back-talked the cops. Tone could not afford a lawyer. He used to give my name and number to the public defender so I could vouch for his job status. I have spent my share of time observing court cases in Harm City, and for all of the overloaded dysfunction, counsel and judge alike seem committed to keeping non-violent employed black men out of jail. They, unlike the people who make the laws, understand that having a job is a huge leg up for men like Tone.

There was an occasion where my night crew staged a mutiny, which resulted in me firing or demoting all but one man. I cobbled together my customer service clerks like Tone and tossed them all onto the night crew for training. I knew this would be tough for Tone, working a full 8 and sometimes 10 hours, as he had a drinking problem. Liquor was how he had swallowed the pain of running the gauntlet between criminals and cops for 40 years in a world that literally did not add up for him, and was plastered with signs that made less sense to him than they do for anyone reading this. He ate a whole lot of pain, and it showed in his eyes. I did not think he would be able to handle the demands of night work, but he wanted the chance to prove himself after I found out he could not count well enough to do the receiving.

Some of the guys on this ad hoc crew hated each other. I assigned them aisles and left them to sort the order without assigning a lead. Sorting the order is what separates the men from the boys on a night crew. Every man needs to be dedicated to saving the next man a step. As I was up in the office taking off my douche bag management drone shirt and tie and slacks and putting on some working clothes, a heated argument broke out between three of the men over how the order would be sorted.

I did not hear Tone's voice.

Two of these dudes were ready to fight, and Joe-Damn barked in his gravelly voice, "Come on ya'll fools. Just aks Jimmy L when his ass get down here."

Then I heard Tone speak up, "No! We men. We gotta learn ta work togetha. Havin' the GM work over night with us is an embarrassment! We need ta come togetha as a crew. No fightin' ya'll—none, not while I'm here."

Tone had always been the quiet man that said "Yes sir," and leant a hand. These guys were dumbfounded, and listened as he laid out a plan that was fair, not too inefficient and had the virtue of simplicity.

I opened the door and came down into the stockroom in my sleeveless shirt and jeans, and he looked at me and said, "We got it covered Boss."

I said, "Then I'll build the displays while you guys freight."

He looked at me and said, "How 'bout I build the displays and you go home and get some rest?"

I just stuck around long enough to make sure Tone had a handle on things. He read at a fifth grade level, could barely count, and was actually drunk at the time. But he had character, had stopped a fight, and had gotten these guys to work together. Now they knew that I trusted him, that as long as they made things work and made him look good, instead of letting him sink—which is what happens to a lot of guys with limited tools that get promoted in retail food—that they all had a job, a boss that would talk to the cops and lawyers on their behalf. They knew, that I knew, that he was drunk. That was actually the glue that sealed the deal with this crew. In my promotion of Tone they had proof that they would only be treated based on their performance, proof that nothing mattered to this version of The Man but actions.

The crew that I had just dissolved had taken a racist stance against working for a white man. This crew, with one of the same men, made an equally cohesive decision to negotiate a work arrangement with that same white man, which was enabled by Tone taking a chance that I would back him up if he stuck his neck out.

Many times I have been party to the unmasking of the toxic chimera of racism in the workplace. So long as the workplace is run on merit, a natural hierarchy based on character will usually emerge. The corporations and unions I have worked for had numerous methods for destroying these natural hierarchies and retarding the working man's experience. But, in a natural work environment, where men have the option of doing the right thing—which is rarely as complicated or as stressful as the alternative—even poorly educated men who have been raised to believe that they are hated and treated unfairly because of their race, will be able to peal the lie away.

I would like to caution the reader that few natural work environments are tolerated in the present society, and that I have never witnessed a mixed gender crew, or an all female crew, uplifting itself in the way that Tone, Joe-Damn, John, and the other men did that night. This was not a one man act. When Tone offered himself as the rallying point, the rest of the crew agreed, and supported him.

Tone was not up to handling this kind of pressure for long, and I eventually gave him an easy gig working daylight so he wouldn't have to worry about man-stomping hoodrats or cops, essentially putting him out to pasture in return for doing his part as a lead over the course of one clutch season.

I don't know what became of Tone's employment status when I left. I do know that he died in his early fifties, this past July, and that his 80-year-old father buried him on a Wednesday.

The Harm City Force Pool
How Many Applicants Out of 45 Were Drug Free and Without Criminal Convictions?

Don't cheat by scrolling to the bottom of the page.

Now guess, of 45 prospective Baltimore County supermarket employees, how many were drug free and without a criminal record?

This morning, after work, I stopped by another Baltimore County supermarket to speak with Bill about his operation. This market is in a sketchy area, but is not half as bad as the true ghetto. It is, however, not too far from the Walmart that lost $600K to theft in the guns and ammo department in 2014, so how good could the prospects be?

Let Bill take it away:

"You would not believe it, Jimmy. I'm looking to fill two openings. How hard can that be? I have forty-five applicants—gotta be able to find somebody decent, right? What do we have a twenty-percent unemployment rate or something, once you factor in the people who are out of work and ran their unemployment benefits dry?

"Okay, after I'm done winnowing out the people who have restricted schedules because they're still serving time, or because of their drug treatment schedule, I'm about halfway through the pile.

"Then I have to toss the applications from people who did not tick off the 'willing and able to pass a drug test' box. That brings me down to maybe ten applications that wouldn't get me laughed out of the office.

"Never mind the qualifications. As far as job skills, sense of urgency and reasonable employment record—nothing, not even worth giving them a try. You think the clerks I have now are lazy—good God!

"So I'm down to two promising applicants, both women, young, able to walk, reasonably articulate and seem to want to work. Now I have to check for criminal records.

"The one girl was discharged from the Army last year, and then immediately commits an armed robbery! Really? If I hire her I might as will hire some thug named Clyde so she'll have help dragging the safe off the dock. A six-year military veteran and you start robbing people as soon as you get out? Has the world gone insane?

"So I pull up the other girl's record. She's twenty-five with five kids. So I guess it makes sense that she has five shoplifting convictions!

"Here I stand, tearing up cardboard—need a job?"

And the answer is—zero!

"Later dude—enjoy!" I said, as he shook his head and looked accusingly at the ceiling.

I didn't even stay long enough to buy the drink I had stopped in for.

'Black Jebus'

On the Road for the Redneck Leg of the Lebron James Imposter Signed Shoe Tour

© 2015 Ishmael

Somewhere in the Rocky Mountains

I was having breakfast with the owner of a cafe, his son and he are chefs. I taught them how to harvest wild mushrooms and other foods in the wild. When I arrived there was a family of blacks eating breakfast, looked like a father about my age with his family, two young men and woman with a couple of tiny girls. The older man came over and thanked Dante for such a fine breakfast, introduced himself as Mike, asked a few questions about the area. We responded and he went back to his table and sat down.

Dante said, "Kind of friendly for a black guy. He must be selling something."

I nodded and went back to eating my breakfast. I noticed a white Mercedes, and Cadillac parked side by side in front of the cafe. To describe the older gentleman he was about 6ft, powerfully built, had on what we call a caddy shack multi-colored golfing hat, gold necklace, t-shirt, Levi's. I finished my breakfast and left.

Okay, fast forward to this morning:

My son-in law and I are eating breakfast, headed for my other job to wire up a pump. He is talking about his week at work and tells me about a funny story of helping a black guy fix his Mercedes at a truck stop about 20 miles from the cafe I just ate at.

I described the guy, and he says, "No shit, how did you know?"

I said, "Was this last Tuesday?" and he nodded, 'yes.'

The guy must have headed east and his radiator hose blew and he had his hood up wondering what to do, told my son-in-law that he didn't know a thing about cars, "should have bought the fucking Cadillac."

My kid and his friend cut the hose down, being enough of it left to reconnect to the radiator. He was praising "Jebus" about the "two angels" that had helped him out.

"Praise Jebus, praise Jebus," he repeated, often.

They finished fixing his car and he offered to buy them each a 6-pack for their services. They declined and told him they had to get back to work. He motioned them over to the his car and told them he was selling basketball shoes personally signed by Lebron James. Now my son-in law and friend had just fixed his car. They had been laughing at the guy while doing the repairs, named him Jebus. So he offers to sell a pair of the shoes to them for just 175 dollars. He said he paid just 100 to acquire them.

My son-in law says, "You are one lousy salesman. How do you know Lebron signed them? And you never tell anyone about the seller's purchase price."

He responded, "My son told me they were signed by Lebron."

My kid said, "If that's true they should be worth thousands of dollars not hundreds. We just fixed your car for free. What the hell else do you want out of us? I think it's time you hit the road."

He had South Carolina plates and had started his so-called sales trip from Oregon.

Thought you might like this story.

Ishmael

PS

Holy section 8! Just dropped some trout off at Dante's. Jebus is back. Must be setting up camp. Had his wife with him according to Dante—steak and eggs. This dude has money. Wonders never cease.

Grant, Tanya and a Twerp
Notes on Our Collective Noose

© 2015 James LaFond

Not long ago I was speaking with an 18-year-old man who described himself as a conservative thinker who wishes to start his own electrical contracting business. Wanting to know what this 18-year-old unicorn had between his ears, I picked a liberal subject, in hopes of finding out where a person of that age, who has just graduated at the top of his class, thinks of State intrusion in family affairs, I told him the following story and asked for his opinion.

A young fighter I know was recently put in a horrible position by his wife, who insisted that he intervene between a strange woman and the child she was spanking in a Laundromat restroom. The man declined to get in a brawl with the strange woman and her boyfriend, and left with his wife as she scolded the spanker for her social sins.

This young, aspiring business man said, "The answer is simple. You get on the phone and call child social services. This option is taught in middle school. That way you don't have to fight the spanker or the thug boyfriend and the situation gets addressed by the authorities."

I offered no opinion, simply wanted to see how a self-described conservative 18-year-old thinks of such things in The People's Republic of Maryland.

Last night I had the opportunity to see where this kind of philosophy gets those low income people who have spent their life under the thumb of Child Protective Services and other such busybody entities.

Grant and Tanya are a young couple in their late twenties who have just begun renting and working out in Baltimore County, having escaped the ghetto. They were "joking around" in the living room when Grant bumped into Tanya playfully and she pushed him with one hand in the same playful manner. Unfortunately, he was off balance already from bumping his narrow ass into her considerable hips, and fell. He put out his hand to break his fall on the wall, and it went through the window instead.

I looked at the picture of Grant's arm before surgery and it looked like he had been mauled by a tiger, his forearm open almost to the bone. Tanya wrapped the wound, applied pressure, got Grant to keep the arm elevated and under pressure, and then drove him to the emergency room.

All Tanya could think about was nerve damage, arterial bleeding, a severed muscle. "Oh God," she said, "What if he can't work because of this—he's supposed to start a new job tomorrow!"

Grant had other things on his mind. How was he going to lie about this? From his experience, being taken to hospitals as a child for injuries stemming from accidents incurred while riding skateboards, climbing vacant houses, riding on bus bumpers, and other stupid shit that boys do, he was worried about Tanya getting locked up. Everyone who grows up in Baltimore City knows that an injury that might have been accused by foul play, spousal abuse, or child abuse, will be investigated and the police notified.

In Grant's mind, if he admitted to staff that Tanya had pushed him, he would not be able to spin it as an accident, with the authority to make that judgment residing with law enforcement personnel. Any act of violence is not a crime against the injured person, but against the State. Grant's fears ranged from having Tanya spend the weekend in jail and losing three shifts worth of pay, to Child Protective Services being called in to investigating their parenting.

While I am of the opinion that Tanya would not be in deep legal trouble for this, since Grant would insist that his injury was the result of an accident, they were both terrified of State intervention in their life, as they had been subjected to government counseling, foster care and family court as children.

So, Grant lied, and told the person investigating his injury at the hospital that he was injured while removing an air conditioner from the living room window.

'The Crappiest Bouncer in Baltimore'
The Hell of Being Straight in Harm City

© 2015 James LaFond

One hot June night as I waited for the #19 bus on Harford road I was approached by a young man, who shouted, "Yo, yo got monay!"

I snarled, shifted my weight, and looked side-to-side, keeping him in my field of vision. He backed off and I boarded.

After I got off the bus at the Inner Harbor I walked through Federal Hill and South Baltimore, infested with crack-heads, meth-heads, coke-heads, and heroin addicts. Panhandling was often used as a cover for attacks in this area. While crossing Fort Avenue two construction workers in a blue pickup truck screamed, "Queer!" and swerved toward me as they drank from bottles of beer.

After my shift the next morning, as I stepped off the bus on Harford and Southern across the street from a rehab clinic, I passed a young man who made hard eye contact with me. He scanned my hands and belt line. I was getting off an out of town bus with work gear on a Saturday morning. I would be carrying cash.

He tried to make eye-contact with me again. I read this as an attempt to initiate a confrontation. I declined, looked around for possible accomplices, and walked past him.

As I passed he rose and turned to follow me up Southern Avenue. That's when I decided to stab him. I shifted my gear into my left hand so that I could draw the screwdriver from the sleeve of the leather knee-pads I carried. I stopped and stared at him. He then stopped advancing and stepped back against the light pole and slumped back down to the ground.

These passing encounters marked a rather typical weekend for me at that time, living in that neighborhood, working that job, around 2000. From 2006 thru 2010, as General Manager of a supermarket in a drug infested area of Northeast Baltimore, I would log up to 20 confrontations per week with panhandling dope fiends on the front sidewalk and parking lot, while my 260 pound security man sat in the office watching live videos of some cashier's big butt. After years of avoiding confrontations I had to initiate them. Then, after 8 hours of aggressive policing in a tie, I'd throw the choker in a locker, slap on a rag and jacket, and become a defender again back out on a bus stop.

My two favorite freaks were Blonde Boy, a sore-covered heroin addict who was built like MMA fighter Tyson Griffin, and Keith of the much-pierced face, who was also blonde, but taller. One evening I was called to the front by an irate woman who claimed she had been panhandled by Blonde Boy. I ran outside, knowing he would still be scavenging for good will. He had an older lady pinned in her car, and was screaming that he needed money. (I think, at this time, my security man was zooming in on Tannika's ample cleavage.) Retail food geek in a tie to the rescue!

I ran up to within five paces of Blonde Boy and stopped. He then turned dramatically, with his hands on the side of his head, his face turning purple, and said, "You, you! You are such an ASSHOLE!!!"

I said, "Yes, that's my job. You have to leave."

He responded, "Why do you have to be such an ASSHOLE!!! I'm sick of you bothering me! Stay away! I'm known for knocking people out!"

I said, "Good, we ought to get along just fine, because I'm known for taking beatings. Come on back to the bus stop and knock me out tonight. But right now, you need to leave."

At this point his mind began processing some violent threat or action, but was short-circuited by the female customer who had complained about him. She had her right arm around my waist and was screaming over my right shoulder while she aimed a container of mace over my left shoulder, all the while pressing her hard nipples into my back. She was screaming, "Die mutherfucker. Starve in a gutter! I'll fuckin' mace your ass."

Thankfully for me she did not spray the mace and blonde boy fled in fear of this little blonde chick who got her rocks off threatening dope-fiends with mace. I then assisted the elderly woman from her car while the psychotic, but actually hot, blonde white-trash chic waited. She told me she liked Italian food, was a single mother, wanted me to beat up her brother, and... somehow I lost interest.

The really great part about this incident, was, when I informed the police that I was becoming tired of Blonde Boy, they went after him—and got Keith instead. Now Keith and Blonde Boy are two of only three blonde men in Baltimore City, so we can forgive the cops. Keith resisted arrest and the cops stomped him out in front of the gay bar down the street.

About 3 months later Keith came to the store front and paced back and forth on the side walk. Apparently my security man had grown bored waiting for the last button on Ashantai's long-suffering undersized blouse to pop, and had done a perimeter walk. He came to me, about ready to have an asthma attack, and said, "Boss, this bad white boy outside. Could you please ask him to go?"

I went outside and dazzled Keith with my eloquence and diction. I think I even called him 'sir.' Keith had been looking to throw down with me. But, upon looking over my shoulder at my sweating and heavily breathing security man, he apparently mistook this adrenaline dump gone bad as the eagerness of a predatory homosexual, and decided to leave.

I could go on for 200 pages about imposing my will on dope-fiends without actually having to touch them. It really is a non-physical art. Out of a probable 1200 panhandler ejections over a 4 year period, I only had to fight with one, and that was over with a single head butt between his eyes.

But still, even after my stint at the Ghetto Grocery Store as the crappiest bouncer in Baltimore, every time I am approached by some parasite that wants me to finance his peculiar form of suicide, a debate rages within me, between my brain and my guts. Should I walk around or stand my ground?

Miss Bette
A Time-Traveling Pioneer Woman Visits Harm City, U.S.A., Disguised as a Cashier

This afternoon I was checking out at a Harm City grocer behind a white couple in their late fifties. The cashier, appearing to be in her 70s, "Miss Bette" as she was called by the oppressed individuals of color working with her, was ringing out their order when she said, to the woman, "Would you like your milk in a bag?"

The woman then turned meekly to her slightly older looking husband, and inquired, "Dear, should we have our milk in a bag?"

Before the man could speak up, Bette, almost through ringing the order and impatient to deal with the milk, snarled, "Don't ask him! What's the matter with you? What will you do when he dies?"

The man and woman looked at her in stunned disbelief, mouths open, while the black lady running the next lane just grinned and whispered, "That's *my* Miss Bette!"

Seemingly not pleased that her point had been made, or would be heeded, Miss Bette snarked, "Oh, don't think it can't happen to you! It happened to me! Look at him, he's getting pretty long in the tooth by my estimation—it could be any time now!"

The woman, and the man, appeared to be shell-shocked, unable to speak, so Miss Bette continued the transaction, and her lecture, "In the bag it goes then. Now listen girly, you need to learn how to do for yourself. My old man up and died on me when I was your age. Now I've got a husband younger than yours. I'm going to die on him just like my first one died on me—so I tell him to do for himself. That'll be forty-eight nineteen, and don't even tell me you're letting him hold the money!"

The woman stepped up and swiped a card, and Miss Bette approved, "That's my girl. Have a nice day."

Miss Bette completely ignored the husband and locked eyes on my, "Step on up, handsome. Do you want your drink in a bag?"

"Whatever you think is best, Miss Bette."

"There you go, Fella, in the bag."

Then, with a glance over her shoulder at the couple walking stiff-legged out the door, she stabbed a thumb in their direction and said, "Can you believe that stupid whore? Jesus, Mary and Joseph! If her old man didn't bolt her head on in the morning she wouldn't be able to find it! Have a nice day now, Fella—come back and see me some time."

And off I walked, with my Bolthouse Farms, 16 ounce mocha protein drink...in a five-gallon bag.

Irene and Dee
Two Dopefiend-Involved Aggressions

© 2015 James LaFond

Irene and Dee were both supermarket security guards I worked with in the late 1990s.

Irene and the Reprobate

#62-06: night, under 10 seconds, first-person defender

"I was coming home from work—waiting for the bus—when this homeless man approached me and asked for a cigarette. I didn't have a cigarette so he cussed me. He had a reprobated mind. I didn't have no weapon so I got up and left. If I hadn't there would have been an altercation."

Dee and the Dopefiend

#62-16: night, minute plus, first-person aggressor

"This man had been pushing a shopping cart with his lady, who had walked out with a loaded backpack. When he came through without a purchase I approached him respectfully and told him he wasn't leaving with that heavy backpack.

He was tall, born in sixty-three, darn near to forty. But he was two feet taller than me and didn't want to go down. I tackled him in the deodorant aisle and we ploughed into the shelf. He wasn't actually trying to hurt me. He just wanted to break free, but I got him cuffed. The police were there within ten minutes.

They wouldn't take him in. He had eighty-six dollars worth of candy in that bag, and we could write-him up for the damaged deodorants. But he had a valid Maryland I.D., and hadn't taken three-hundred dollars worth of product, so he just got a citation.

I treat the shoplifters with respect. They don't get locked up—I mean how is a guy going to run out of a market with three-hundred dollars worth of food? This guy had drug problems, needles in his pockets. It is important that they look at you as a guy who was just doing his job. You don't want somebody coming back to take a shot at you."

A Day At the Baltimore Zoo
Why The Baltimore City Zoo Has Begun To Segregate Primates By Age

© 2015 James LaFond

Today I walked past a hoodrat access trail, which is used for mugging, mob attacks and armed robberies, and mating as well, past which I have been pursued numerous times. I thought I noticed hoodrat scat in the dirt footpath and decided to investigate and determine if they had begun eating humans yet. Then I discovered that these 15 "piles of scat" were indeed 15 handfuls of artificial hair sewn into real hair, much of which was still attacked to the base of the weave. This had obviously been the scene of a female hoodrat combat over mating rights. The orangutan-red hoodrat hair had fallen in three clumps, along with the chimp-black hoodrat hair, with two half handfuls of chimp hair scattered between pile B and C, with the entire length of the clinch running to 30 feet. The final hair pile had more chimp weave with more anchoring natural hair torn out by the roots. Overall handfuls of torn out hair tallied: chimp-black 8, orang-red 7. From these signs I declare the orangutan hoodrat the winner!

Then, upon my return from the scout I received an email from Inspector Ratchet with the following attachments.

Imagine going to all the trouble to retake your teaching exam six times in order to qualify for a job brainwashing hoodrats, only to have them challenge you to fights.

Notice how experienced the young men are at separating and restraining female combatants, and how good that teacher is at the hair-hat locker slam.

Checkout the second video of the psychotic boy-beating teacher. The mother's commentary is telling.

https://youtu.be/OBmDIHXVnTU

http://www.theroot.com/articles/culture/2014/10/watch_ student_charged_with_assault_and_teacher_on_leave_ after_fight_caught.html?wpisrc=ck_facebook_CK- ROOT.ALL-TRF-A02-FB-FBLP-FKW-US-BCULT-BO-18-R12

https://www.youtube.com/watch?v=oGJUddHbpRg

'Getting Around To It'
A Motivational Tool From the 1970s

Last week, my supervisor was complaining to me about his information gatekeepers, the "scanning department." In any grocery store these people are the slacker elite, denying tag and sign requests from the lowly peasant class that do not have the access code or ability to use the pricing machinery that drives store sales. I ruled my scanning crew with an iron fist—and with humor as well, though it often went unappreciated. When I would walk into their office early, or on my day off, or after I had left for the day, a collective groan would fill the air.

Now, as a lowly clerk, I am once again at their mercy, unable to move new or overstocked items before they go out of date for lack of a sign.

It is the way of the retail food world.

But Joe had had enough, and complained to me, asking my advice about what to do with an employee that answered his request for a sale sign with, "I'll take care of it when I get around to it," before returning to her non-work related gossip.

Remembering an invention of my father, Ted LaFond, who managed a print shop in the 1970s, I employed my box cutter and pen on a sheet of cardboard, and in minutes armed my boss with three rounds of anti-slacker ammunition. They were not printed on 20-bond Hamermill like Dad's, but they would do.

He now had in his hands three round cardboard disks, inscribed with "To-It."

For now on, he need only hand out the missing round To-It to his procrastinating scanners and all will be well.

Being Eaten Alive On The Job
When Your Job Sucks: A Quarter Hour As A Pimp Collecting Drug Money

© 2015 James LaFond

Lazarus is a tall heavily built black man who runs a string of hookers for high end guys and sells quality weed and powder cocaine to the customers as well. He decided to branch out into wholesaling a little. He used a gun for home defense but did not pack one on him. A retailer of his, in an area of the city bordering the suburbs, where there were more vacant houses than occupied lots, was in need of a pep talk on cooperation, timely payments, and other such aspects of team play. Lazarus liked to handle things with a light touch.

#10-02: day, minutes, first-person defender

Lazarus decided to walk past the building, doing a circuit of the row to ascertain the situation, before approaching the front door. He was walking past an adjacent rundown rental property when he was attacked by a pit bull. The thing leaped for his throat and he presented his left forearm, which was seized between two vice-like rows of teeth.

What surprised him was that the dog, at perhaps a quarter of his weight, was able to drag him around. It quickly wrestled him to the ground. The dog's grip slid down from the forearm, leaving it half-skinned, to the hand, and would not let go. As the dog literally ate his left hand the big man methodically broke the dog's legs with his right hand. This took a few minutes by his estimation, "the length of a song."

With four broken legs, the dog doggedly hung on—PETA forgive me, but I had to—but was no longer able to drag or even tug on Lazarus' arm. The dog kept eating though. It took Lazarus another few minutes to drag the twisting munching critter across the overgrown lot, both of them prone, as the dog would curl and roll around his hand when he tried to rise. He managed to drag himself and the dog within reach of a two-by-four, which he used to beat the dog, flattening out the base of its skull and then breaking the back of the neck, not all too concerned about smashing his half-eaten left hand along with its head.

The dog died anticlimactically and released his hand. He had been afraid that he would have to smash the snout to get his hand out, but the pit bull did not maintain the death grip he had feared.

Lazarus lost the two small fingers of the left hand, and 20 years later is still pimping and dealing weed, recently taking a trip oversees to procure some choice seed for his grower.

10:04 in the morning and I have cop cruisers roaring down the street.

'My Ride Home'
Columbine Joe, the Trash Man

© 2015 James LaFond

When I was twenty-four I had this job working on a trash truck up in Whitehall—north of Towson up near the Pennsylvania state line. I didn't drive—didn't even have my license. I was done with the drug scene, trying to get a new start. The area was real wide open, lots of property, wooded areas. However, it was a long walk home.

One day, after work, this older guy, a coworker—he looked like he was in his late forties or early fifties, but might have been younger based on his lifestyle—offered to give me a ride home. He does tell me that he has something he has to take care of. He drives me to this remote wooded location, gets out of the truck—it was a white pickup truck. I think you had to have a white pickup truck to live in Whitehall, like it's freagin' law or something.

Anyway, he starts to walk off into the woods and tells me to get behind the wheel. I'm like, "Dude, I don't even drive!"

I'm just sitting there, for like twenty minutes, I suppose. Then he comes running out of the woods yelling for me to start it up and drive. I reiterated the fact of my lack of driving experience and license, so he yells at me to slide into the passenger seat. As he starts it up that's when I hear the helicopter, and then see it, a police helicopter looking for his ass. He is driving like a maniac, and sometimes pulling over and hiding too. He knew what he was doing. But I had watched cops [the syndicated TV show] a lot, and had no faith in him getting away from a helicopter. I'm also remembering from the cops show that when there is a passenger they treat him like he's guilty too. So I'm like, great, I'm going to get my ass kicked and get locked up, or better yet, die in a high speed crash.

You know, I still can't believe it, but he lost the chopper. They had staked out his plants and waited for him to show up. But he knew the byways and back ways of Whitehall.

Now, when he dropped me off, I said, "Dude, tomorrow I'm walking home, okay."

'The Way of the World'
Columbine Joe, the Liquor Store Clerk

© 2015 James LaFond

Okay, you promised a book, and I want a book—something funny to show the kids and whatnot—but I've got to give up the cruddy stuff too?

[Frowns, strokes beard, shakes head "no" then nods head "yes"]

Okay—let's see if we can be really general—generously general on the time frame here, since, when this happened, I officially had my act together and had come to Jesus.

[Rubs beard as author gives blatantly false assurances]

Darn, brother, this is hard. Have to pity those Catholics. It's one thing to come clean with the Lord, but—darn, okay.

I was divorced, working in a liquor store making seven dollars an hour—and mind you this wasn't that long ago. Seven bucks an hour does not go far. And the ex-wife has them taking a ridiculous amount of child support out of me. I'm literally making less than my child support. Forget garnishment, that would never cover it, bro. I had to pay the lawyer, every month, or, go, to, jail!

The world is the world and I was living in it—and thankfully still am. Hopefully the Lord understands.

I'm working behind the counter at the liquor store making seven an hour, so what else can I do but sell weed? It's the same customer base. I don't have the stuff on me—it's behind some bottle of gin that never sells.

I tell the customers—my private customers—that they have to buy something from the store—which is only fair because I am on the owner's space and time, and is prudent besides. So I was generating tax revenue, and volume for my employer. They would come in, buy a forty for two bucks, drop a ten on me, and would be out the door with a little something extra.

After a while it turned into real money—after a little while I should say. It didn't take long. People find you. So, honestly, even after partaking a might myself, I was still making multiple times more in cash than I was on the job. The system was basically making me do it. I either I go to jail or make money—a lot more money than I'd ever make working a job—to make the child support.

[Extends open hand like he is pushing on a door to test it]

Now, you would think—a lawyer being sharper than the ordinary tool—that this lawyer would know, based on the amount of cash, and the denominations that I was bringing to him, where the money was coming from. So, this lawyer will wash my money for free as long as he's getting his piece of the action.

After a while I started moving other stuff for associates, mostly powder. I prefer the powder because you can cook it up, sell it as rock, and make a big profit, where, with the pills, it's pretty much like selling beans.

Then I got engaged.

[Stands back, strokes beard, nods with scrunched face]

There can't be any secrets in a true union. So I told my fiancé. When she found out how much I was making she got nervous—so I stopped. I did, though, pay for the wedding with the proceeds, put that money into a church.

The world is the world, brother.

Evil Construction
Ishmael: Almost My Worst Job

In the 1980s with the economy bad, the mine I worked at had shut down for good, real-estate had went crazy in Park City. With all the building going on I took a job pouring cement. I worked for a fly by night construction company. My friend and I called it Evil construction. Some of the bikers we worked with ran a chop shop at night. My friend and I didn't do drugs, just booze; we kept our heads down drawing a paycheck looking for something better.

These guys hated our guts, making fun of our rural backgrounds. They were lazy bastards too, we did most of the form work, and cement pours. One biker locked his kid in the basement for scratching his bike. I mentally murdered the asshole every time I spoke to him. He was finally arrested for possession of stolen property. Hope he made the "point of the mountain," our state prison, and some skin head was using him for a pin cushion. We quit that fall, and I headed for the oilfield. I didn't know then that a place could be worse than that.

'These Murdering Pair of Mutts'
Ishmael on the Yuppie Invasion of Rural America

© 2015 Ishmael

"Here's a story for you before I forget again."

"Back in my teens and early 20s, people were moving in from the city and buying up farm property along the foothills. These were major wintering areas for Elk and Mule Deer. They would let their dogs run free.

"In February and March the snow would get a crust on it. The Deer, usually does and fawns, would break through and were easy prey for the predators, snow being three to four feet deep. Some of the dogs would develop a taste for venison. They would kill one and move on to the next like it was a sport.

"The old game warden couldn't keep up with the work load, and I had young legs, so any problem dogs were assigned to Shayne and I. We would get up above the deer early in the morning before the sun warmed up the snow and hunt dogs. The dogs would show up about the time the crust would thaw. Remember the leash law was enforced then, big game and livestock were protected."

"One **city savage** had these murdering pair of mutts. He had paid, according to his bragging, 500 dollars a piece for them. Of course they never left his property. Well it was sure fun leaving them dead for the buzzards—1000 dollars of dog meat, laying next to a bunch of deer they had killed. But the thing that stays in my mind, was the domestic dogs killed more viciously than coyotes, reminds me of civilized humans."

-Ishmael

Robert E. Howard had his Conan character say something like this in most of the stories he wrote on this subject of civilization versus barbarism. Edgar Rice Burroughs made similar observations through his Tarzan character. My idea is that feral humans are more vicious than undomesticated types because they carry more fear, and less knowledge, of aggression, and yet live in a society suffused in—indeed based on—aggression. As far as human-on-human cruelty, ritualized—not personal, but tribal—torture is a primal feature in some warlike societies, that does offer a caveat to this observation.

'If The Heart is Compassionate the Hand Fails'
Notes from Medieval Araby from Jinn Joe: Samuel L. Jackson's Part Time Job

© 2015 James LaFond

Once upon a bloody time Jinn Joe managed to get a hold of a flying carpet in 1201, during the cannibal rampage in Misr, just up the Harvester's Sickle Road from Cairo, and fortunately managed to pilot it to Masada, breaking through a dimension door into 2015, where he has been spying for the readers of jameslafond.com from a hidden vault. As a Jinn who once upon a time helped troubled little boys with their problems escaping tyrants and wizards and such, Jinn Joe was somewhat bothered by the recently posted video **'Drop-Kicking Toddlers'** in which a boy is seen abusing toddlers. The boy is of course, black, which seems to be the preferred race that governments use to attack their population.

"I couldn't watch the video of the black kid kicking around black toddlers. In general, I think the Muslims may have been onto something when they used the [black] men for eunuch slave labor and the better looking women for concubines. They also apparently used blacks to populate malarial oases, which nobody else could inhabit. To this day, the Saudis use a black executioner: https://youtu.be/UxmBp23W6nc

"Also, Prince Bandar, who ran Saudi's intelligence work with/in the US and apparently is responsible for a lot of the American debacle in the Middle East over the last decade, is the son of a black concubine, which makes him ineligible for the throne but quite useful for doing dirty work:
https://en.wikipedia.org/wiki/Bandar_bin_Sultan

I was thrilled to recognize the Saudi executioner as Samuel L. Jackson!

Thanks Joe!

The interviews with the black headsmen are fascinating windows into the medieval mindset. I do have one point of agreement with Islamic law. If a significant number of Saudi women are as good looking as the unveiled newscaster, then I understand the need for covering their face.

https://youtu.be/UxmBp23W6nc

'Mamma, Wait!'
An Exceptionally Well-Equipped Shoplifting Attempt

© 2016 James LaFond

As I was heading down to the local ghetto grocer for my milk, crossing the parcel pickup area, a very, very large black woman was pushing a cart of groceries out into the Sunday afternoon air. She was about five feet ten inches and perhaps 450 pounds, with breasts the size of an NFL helmet, dressed in stretchy tiger-stripe pants and shirt, with a purple ruffled vest and knee high vinyl hooker boots.

Behind her came the Nigerian security guard shouting, "Mamma, Mamma, wait. Stop, Mamma, I must have what is in your shirt!"

The woman stopped, turned like a tigress at bay and snarled menacingly at the 160 pound middle-aged man, who skipped forward on tip toe like he was trying to reach his hand into a tank of swarming hornets. Like a veritable Mowgli he deftly inserted his hand into the gargantuan cleavage before the creature could engulf him in her beastly embrace and withdrew a two pound box of frozen hamburger patties from between the woman's breasts!

As she scowled, and he skipped away sprite-like with joy, said, "Have a nice day, Mamma, come again."

Meanwhile, Mister Lee, the hacker on duty, said, "Good Lord, ain't nobody want to buy them funky burgers now!"

Improvise!
O Hayes Odyssey

I have occasionally known people for whom working a job is just a break—a temporary setback. Oliver is one of those men, a born entrepreneur with a scathing disdain for the slave mentality he encounters in everyday life.

"I was born in Kingston Jamaica and came here as a boy. My father was Jamaican and my mother English. My family in England says blacks get treated better over there, but there ain't shit over there. Jamaica is just crazy. I'm going down there this summer to straighten out something for my grandmother, who some people are not dealing squarely with. I'm not going alone. I have citizenship in all three counties, so I have thought about drifting, picking up and moving as the places fall apart.

"My cousin came to America with me—the same age. His mother got a six-figure job right off the bat. My mother struggled but did well, as did my father, but he's not all about supporting the family."

[Oliver has custody of both of his children, mentors his two little sisters, buys his mother a car when she needs one and fixes it when she breaks it, and has just bought his oldest younger sister a car, having assumed a patriarchal role for himself in a society where that is taboo for a man of his race.]

"When you come from Jamaica the schooling here is so bad, so primitive, that it's actually hard to fit in. My older sister was twelve and tested out at college level. What did they do—put her in her age grade so she could suffer with all of those dummies. I don't believe in school and refuse to send my children to pre-school. I'm teaching them to read myself. Hopefully I'll do well enough in business to school them myself and avoid the Stupidity Factory.

"You know, I've come to the conclusion that adults who believe that street-fighting is a good idea have something wrong with their minds. But when I was a kid, and I first met a white person, I was shocked to discover that people outside of the black urban environment do not fight all of the time! It was a real wakeup call. Like, 'Wow, no wonder we don't have shit!'

"My cousin had everything, grew up with all the best clothes, latest video games, most expensive sneakers under the Christmas tree. Me, I didn't have shit. When we were thirteen I go to the dollar store with him and he tries to rob it! Tries to stick up the clerk, without a gun, when he doesn't have a want in the world. It is as if society told him he is supposed to be a jackass and so he does.

"I have this friend who is the opposite—same thing, no father in his life—with a mother that looks like Mike Tyson, who either beats his ass or babies him. We're in his car and he runs out of gas and wants to call his mother! 'Are you kiddin' me, Nigga!' I said, 'Motherfucker, improvise! Get out and walk to the gas station.'

"Everybody I know, they step out from their mother and know they can return if it doesn't work out. For me, that's unthinkable. I'm a man. I'll be homeless before I live as a boy again. But most of these motherfuckers don't care, they just want to be violent boys, who can't even fight their way clear of a serious situation. It's a recipe for disaster.

"I was broke with no job and only twenty bucks. I bought an auto part, refurbished it, and sold it for two hundred, then kept trading up until I got a car without a hood, and sold that bitch twice—repossessed it from the one non-paying motherfucker and sold it again. I just don't see how you submit to being a woman's bitch.

"I used to believe the axiom "niggers can't have shit," even when I was selling cars for these thieves that were ripping people off. I knew I was going to have to quit that business because it was unethical, so invested in this one customer's real estate business after he bought a vehicle with a bag of money—fifty-grand in a bag. That guy convinced me that I can make it. If I go back into selling cars it will be on my own. I always make 500 percent or more on a car. I want to work up to where I can buy a house on a property big enough to hunt on, and I'm not going to do that blaming the world and doing stupid shit.

"The problem is making money takes up time you need for important stuff like fighting and training and reading and writing. So it's like a long slow tunnel to the other side. How is it on the other side, James? How did stepping away from earning work out for you?"

[To paraphrase and condense my answer: Great, but was only possible after getting my sons off into the world, and I read over 2,000 books while immersed in the working world, and learned things about people while there, so it was not a wasted effort, even in existential terms.]

"Thanks, James. That really helps. Measuring my means and my aspirations gets tricky sometimes. Hopefully this latest venture gets me the income and the time to support my family and work on what matters. I'm looking forward to reading with my kids, them reading a book while I'm reading a book, and discussing the subject matter."

Mister Barth
When Your Job Sucks, But You Have Control of the Radio

© 2016 James LaFond

When I was sixteen and had just dropped out of high school, I began working at Mancuso Printing in Washington PA, in the bindery, which meant that my job consisted of standing before a series of boards that circled the room, stacked on cinder blocks. On these boards, along the east, south and west wall, were stacked 370-some stacks of printed paper that consisted of the Fox Groceries pull-tab catalog, to be collated and spirally bound. I collated, which meant I placed page 1 on top of page 2, and those on top of page 3, and those on top of page 4 and those on top of page 5!

"Aghhhh!"

Most of the presses were small offset presses, one of which was run by an 18-year-old guy who had the radio! Thankfully we both liked rock, and so did my partner, Peter Dan, a former drug addict of perhaps 25 who told me stories about getting kicked out of whorehouses, gangbanging biker babes and having sex with sheep in hip wader boots, so that you could jam the sheep's legs down in the boots and she would be stuck, and move around like she liked you as well.

The big Hiedleburg press was run by Mister Barth, a tall, bearded, older German man who had just immigrated from Bolivia. As a WWII buff I was somewhat afraid of this fellow. Mister Barth hated the rock music and took refuge in the noise of the monstrous machine he cared for. But the ink and paper would need changed and the offset press kid would crank up the music, to which Mister Barth would grumble under his breath in German.

A popular song of the time was ZZ Top's La Grange, a song that finally won the old German refugee over to rock and roll. One day, Peter Dan nudged me and said, "Holy Shit, Herr Hiedleburg is doing the Texas Boogie," and we were treated to Mister Barth—all six foot four inches of his silver-bearded propriety growling, "Eh hehehe!" and dancing slowly about the big press grumbling the lyrics to the tune below.

ZZ Top La Grange live 1982

https://www.youtube.com/watch?v=SE1xO44FlME

'The Poleese Be Around'
Driving the Sedan Surreal

Mobali is a Nigerian man who is a slight, mild-mannered man with a kind disposition. he seems genuinely bemused by Baltimore, and objects when one asks him what it is like to drive a cab.

"Oh, not I, only Uber. I could not subsist if I was required to extract money from my customers. They make the call with their credit card and the fee is deducted. I could not exchange money with these people—It would be far too perilous. This is a trying place. I only wish I knew the good areas and the bad, so I could decline more calls. Some of the places I drive to are such that I would never accept the call if only I knew what the area was like.

"The one woman, gets into the car with her two children and looks down at her smart phone the entire ride as I take her to the address she placed in the GPS tracker. I stop so that they could get out and she looks up, and gets nasty, saying, "Why are you dropping me off here. I do not get off here.'

"I said, 'Miss, this was the address you entered. Look, it is right here on the GPS.'

"She then says, 'You should have asked me for directions!'

"I said, 'But Miss, I did, and you gave me these directions. Besides, if I may, had you been paying attention to the route and your children, you might have been able to advise me to adjust the route to your liking.'

"And she was off in a huff, hauling her young ones down the street.

"Then, last night, I receive a booking for a customer at a location I have not been to. This place, when I arrive there, seemed bad. I am required to wait for five minutes. After five minutes, I drive around the block, coming back, and call her, to alert her to the fact that I am about to leave. She is eager that I not leave, saying that she sees my car, but is afraid to come out of her front door because, 'The poleese be around,' wanting me to drive down to the end of the block so that she can come out the back way!

"Oh no, if it is a bad thing to have the poleese around then it is not the area I wish to do business in! When your internet map of Baltimore becomes available I shall assuredly use it."

'Sweating It on the Side of the Road'
Squashing Cops with Thomas in a 16-Ton Mack Truck

© 2016 James LaFond

"This was a few years back when I was driving for the furniture company. I drove a twenty-six-thousand-pound, straight, Mack truck, with an over cab—so the engine was not sticking out front. I was driving in the face of the truck like a bus. One more pound and I would have needed a CDL license. Don't get me wrong, it's a big truck, and was loaded with about sixteen-thousand pounds worth of furniture.

"This was down in Anne Arundel County and it was raining terribly. I was behind an unmarked cop car, with two plain clothes cops in the front seat, and some guy in the back seat. The car had Virginia plates. These were Virginia cops. He had two cars in front of him that had their turn signals on and he was giving them space. I gave him fifty yards. We were doing forty. The rain was coming down so hard it was difficult to see. The road was also in bad condition, and had these divots in it filled with water.

"Well, I thought he was going through the yellow light. Cops always take the yellow light. But he stops. I put on the air brake and nothing. If it was dry, no problem. I look to the right—trees. I look to the left, cars. I hit the horn and the guy in the back seat looks up at me with the biggest eyes. He was in shock. I rammed him right through the intersection. The entire back of the car was an accordion, all the way up to the back window, which just folded.

"I was terrified. The funny thing is, we had a flat counter between the seats were we set our drinks. Mine didn't even spill. We hardly felt a thing. The guy in the back seat is fine. The driver folded up the wheel, bent it forward in a U. The passenger was banged up, he's on his phone calling, cops are coming, and coming, and coming, ambulances, a tow truck. The entire time I'm sweating it on the side of the road, in the rain, my hood up, standing there waiting to be charged.

"My helper, he had a bench warrant out for his arrest. So he calls up his girl and she comes and picks him up while the cops are there. Not a single cop said anything to me.

"The passenger goes off in an ambulance.

"The driver, he was in bad shape. They strap him into another ambulance.

"The guy in the back seat, he drives off in the back of another un-marked car—no handcuffs. He didn't try to run.

"They crack the trunk and take away the guns.

"More cops leave, not a one of them having asked or said a thing. I did not even have to present my license.

"The car is towed, and the rest of the cops leave, and there I am standing on the side of the road.

"I didn't realize how bad the truck was because it was raining. I drove home. Then when I drove back into work the next day it started to overheat. The radiator had been blown, but the rain kept the engine cool.

"A few months later we get a call from the Anne Arundel County police, and they want to know what truck it was, what driver it was, and want our information. We didn't know anything—nothing. No detectives every came to the store.

"I have no idea what that was about. Were they drunk? Were they doing something they weren't supposed to do? Was it witness protection, an extradition? All I know is that I've never been so scared and never got so lucky."

-Thomas

These Whiney Children?
A Man Question from Ishmael

"Woodstock and I were talking about becoming "Dinosaurs" at work, in the past we have both held positions of leadership. We have a PC liberal as a general manager, a post I held 20 yrs ago at a different employment, I see more manginas holding positions of leadership, you look cross-eyed at these younger men and they run to a supervisor crying about being bullied, even if you offer patient criticism at their lazy work ethic. Woodstock and I use to take a drive and argue all the time, blow off steam and still remain friends. WTH is wrong with these whiney children?"

Ishmael.

Brother, this generation of males are not producing men above 5%. Last Wednesday I sat during my break and watched my middle-aged white conservative supervisor argue with a 20-year old black liberal clerk about "Cops lives matter" and "black lives matter."

They are both thoroughly immersed in the gossipy world of women. At least the old guy knows it and chaffs at the scented chains. But the young dude had no idea that he is exactly what a woman his age was thirty years ago, right down to the C-cups.

This generation has wider hips and narrower shoulders than the last, walk up on their feet like sissies, and are sissies!

What was really great was when I walked up to the 20-year-old black mangina and said,

"You know, Mister Ron does not like the fact that I hate the cops, and still hate them as their bodies get carted by on that railroad [two slain cops were trained through our location for burial in the middle of the night wed/thur], but he deals with it because he knows I live in the city and figures I have my reasons. Do you know what my reasons are, Malcolm?"

Malcolm, whom I coach on his writing, and really is trying to be the best man he can in the feminine context he was born, said, with a look of wide fright on his face, "No, why?"

"Because they prevent me from defending myself, from slaughtering the packs of hood rats that threaten and menace me and who should be fed to the crows."

"Wow, that, that, that's really intense man—I gotta get back to—talk to you later Mister Jimmy," and off he ran seeking the place in his mind where everything will be just fine provided you let the government know how you feel, so they can work on a solution.

Ishmael, this kid is one of the only young dudes that can talk to me without cringing or running, of about a dozen college age kids at work. It is as if they have a testosterone allergy. You know, it's a good thing I have a hernia or two, otherwise I'd be tempted to corral all of the plump young Phillies these colts aren't horse enough to satisfy. They won't even have to be gelded!

Seriously, man, as a coach, I see lack of testosterone across the racial divides. It is worse among the backs. Seriously, we have pack attacks in such large volume because theses sissy black boys, raised by women and video games, know that their granddaddy was feared by white men, and want that "respect" as well. So, in light of their near total lack of rugged manliness, they pack up and attack like wayward chimps.

The point is Mister Ron, who had more reason to be offended by my stance than Malcolm did, looked me right in the eye, and said, "I disagree with your point, but understand. It's a hard world. I guess as long as you understand that its hard for the cops too, then we have a place to stand together."

But the young guy was just floored by my unilateral, individual, aggression, could not really process a sense of animosity that deep that was not a collective guilt-bias of some kind. What is most terrible about this cultural womanization of a generation, is that it prevents a young man grown old to express the wisdom that Mister Ron did, despite being upset. Our young men are coming into life psychologically disabled, which is what our masters want.

As the new maleness would seek not to offend, "I feel your pain, sibling."

My Father
A Reader, on Our Worldly Purpose

My father died 20 years ago this month, his massive barrel chest had shrunk to teenage proportions. His tree trunk legs looked like dead saplings. I watched him die in inches for 10 years. He had been a Roughneck, Sheepherder, Hard Rock Miner, Amateur Boxer, Saddle Bronc rider.

My slightly insane mother was forever chewing his tired butt. She never recovered from seeing my brother mangled on the highway.

This chapter in your book brings back visions of my youth. My father died penniless, but he was one of the finest humans I know—worked to death, broken, by the same fucking bankrupted, soulless, money changers of materialism. I'm damn proud of my low station in life.

Work to the top, yes—then strangle the bastards.

-Anonymously yours

When Your Boss Sucks
Defining The Management Mangina With Samuel Finlay

"I have a disagreement with something you mentioned about unions and management. I'm in a union and every manager I've worked for has been a brown nosed, back-stabbing, spineless mangina. I think its part of management culture in corporations to promote this type exclusively. Easily led, easily terrified of losing face, pathetic creatures. Your experience may differ."

-Sam

Sam, our experience does not seem to differ much. The management creature you describe has generally been the one holding the reins of the union carriage I was yoked to.

First, I do believe that unions are necessary and desirable for trades, and do have two friends who have had all good experiences as union electricians.

Sam, you have probably taken offense to one of my many anti-union statements. I was in management for four years and in a union for 15. The entire time I was in the union I turned down management positions because I knew I would be unable to reward good employees. If I had a guy stocking 400 pieces a night I would not be allowed to pay him anymore than the guy freighting 45 pieces, as United Food and Commercial Workers Local 27 was a communist entity that stipulated that merit pay was not a management option. This was one of the few things they took a stand on. That union currently has [I think] seven contract tiers for the same classifications. I used to work in an aisle with a guy making 18 an hour who did nothing next to another guy who made 7.50 an hour, who was expected not to be demoralized by the fact that his salary capped at 10.40!

What was worse is that this union sold future employees out with every contract, giving the company most of what it wanted and getting current union members to vote for lower pay for future union members. The other thing they did, was get in lockstep with management to eliminate fulltime positions! By eliminating full time employment the company would have to hire twice as many people and the union would make more money, as the number of union members increased!

When I had a hearing for a suspension caused by store level management lying about me, I noticed that the female union rep came in with the Vice President, and head of HR, Mike Deagro—in Mike's imported car, the dapper Italian and the fawning young lady, who he had breakfast and lunch with. I ignored her, other than to check out her ass and pretty face so that Mike knew he and I were on the same page, and then preceded to destroy my manager, who got demoted and transferred, with me offered his position. It was Mike and Me. I didn't need his arm candy mouthing platitudes. She was just a piece of union ass. Mike was The Man, and I was Mike's best man, and he knew it. But, he would not have known it had I not been able to converse outside of the adversarial union versus management box.

The worst thing about working in union retail outlets was the toxic relationship that the adversarial union versus management structure produced. Employees made lack of productivity an ethos. The employers, unable to reward a good worker with anything other than a management position—which open but rarely— resorted to exactly the type of manipulative, back-stabbing negative supervision you are describing.

I have worked in 4 non-union food markets as an employee. Three of these operations had management staff who encouraged, rewarded and helped me. The bad outfit, I eventually came back to as a GM and addressed those issues. In the four unionized chain stores I worked as an employee [as opposed to a consultant or vender] all were negative experiences, and remained so as new managers came and went, for the most part interchangeable black-tie cookies stamped from the same corporate cutter—many of them thieves. I was able to form positive relationships with key management figures by being very productive and gaining intangible benefits such as one redneck manager telling his redneck night captain, who had just written me up for being late, "Don't fuck with my fuckin' hippie, boy! My fuckin hippie is worth three men—fuckin' throw that fuckin' write up in the fuckin' trash you fuckin' idiot."

Such "on the sly" rewards earned me the undying hatred of my union coworkers, who would even threaten me on occasion. Oddly enough, at the last store I was stationed, I became an informal shop steward, a mediator between management and the staff. Because the shop steward only held that position so he would have super seniority, and did not care about his fellow union members, which was very common. Rarely was the shop steward trusted, and often did they betray that trust they had been given. With the managers you knew going in that they were manipulative, backstabbing savages with no morality. But the shop steward was the snake in the grass.

Granted, retail food is the pits, so I expect everybody to be a pit-level person, and it is not right for me to categorize all unions like this low rent one.

One thing that did really bother me about the Teamsters union was the following, which is a perfect illustration of how the negative union mentality is triggered by the manipulative management mentality, which is set in motion by the adversarial nature of the union-management relationship:

When Your Job Sucks

When my brother worked for UPS, he was low man, so got the Reisterstown Road Route, where guys did not last because they were constantly robbed at gunpoint. Tony decided to max his speed on this route, was the first guy out the chute and literally ran through his stops. Tony did so good, that he came to the attention of management, who went to the other drivers and demanded they work as hard as Tony. So the other drivers blocked him in for two hours in the morning, literally putting him in hoodrat gun sights. He soon quit rather than get stuck up on a regular basis.

Overall, I think unions function better in the trades because they are still set up as brotherhoods and take part in preserving the trade skill set, as guilds of old did. I think unions are a mistake in menial occupations, in which they are just vehicles for collective job security that enable low productivity. Union supermarkets are continuing to diminish because of this. I think that a union is something that calls for high level members, and a guild organization committed to upholding trade standards, not lowering them.

As for your description of management as "brown nosed, back-stabbing, spineless mangina," in my experience, 60-70% of managers in non-union settings fit this mold, and that in union settings, 90+% fit this poor mold.

Sam, this deserves more space than I gave it here, and is a symptom of a larger problem, namely our increasingly feminized men, and the fact that men who now wish to advance in management, are often selected for their passive-aggressive, pecking-order-focused, feminine traits, as the traits of submissive, natural slaves—who will demand likewise empty-headed compliance from those beneath them—are desired by the upper echelons of management, who wish to preserve the male role for themselves, even at the expense of function and profit, for this style of management does not grow a vibrant business, but rather a structure built on a self-destructive foundation.

Thanks, Sam, for getting my brain ticking this afternoon.

'If the Minimum Wage is Increased to $15'

'What Would Happen in the Retail Food Business?': A Man Question from Patrick

© 2016 James LaFond

Traditional retail food outlets profit at year's end, 50 cents to $2 of every $100 they ring on the register, excluding sales taxes. As many as half of all chain stores do not generate any profit, often losing money. Essentially, supermarkets are penny businesses that manage to do little more than support one low six-figure salary for a director, a dozen lower middleclass employees, and as many as a hundred-and-twenty poverty line employees living from check to check. The slim profits are generally needed to cover slip and fall law suits, equipment replacement and software upgrades.

Wholesalers do better.

Manufacturers make the lion's share.

Most supermarkets are now owned by wholesalers, who make little or no profit as retail outlets but serve as outlets for wholesale merchandise.

In the Baltimore area the typical grocer employees 100 clerks of various types.

Of this 100, 20 are full time employees, who are "leads" making between $12-16 per hour, with few toping $14 an hour. These people do 80% of the work. They make it happen.

80 of the 100 employees are part timers making between 8 and 11 per an hour, and rarely worth that. These 80 people only do 20% of the work, which is something the liberal mind cannot wrap its head around until it has been put to work with its hands. Primarily, these people are there for customer service—getting your order checked out—and trying to take some of the burden off of the real producers, who are the only ones that move significant merchandise.

If the $15 minimum wage hit, and I was running a market, raising prices would put me out of business, because the big outfits would hold out on the old price line and eat the loss to wait for smaller outfits to go under, and then makeup for their diminished profit by acquiring this extra market share and by raising prices after acquiring that market share.

So, regional, local and marginal chains [which describes most food retailers]—if they wanted to ride it out until Walmart and Wegemens and Safeway jacked their prices up, would:

-lay off half of the part-time staff

-put wage caps on full time employees, including a ban on overtime

-to pay for the unemployment insurance bill part-timers who remained would all be cut to the minimum legal hours, down to 4, 8 or 16 per week depending on state and contract.

-stock levels would be reduced by roughly 50 percent

-retailers would begin selling more space to DSD outfits, such as soda and potato chip companies, who merchandise their own goods.

-For the long haul there would be a hiring freeze and further staff reductions as the labor intensive shelf set was dismantled and converted to box display. My eventual goal would look like an Aldi's employing five to ten employees instead of a hundred. The additional workload on the demoralized leads, knowing that they would never receive a pay increase, and that every consumer good was now going to cost them more, would enable me to achieve this through attrition as they became "sick," made disability claims based on the aches and pains they are already plagued with and which would be exasperated by the increased workload, would enable a much leaner operation, that would hopefully be able to survive in the changing marketplace.

Actually, Patrick, I hope this does happen. Because I will be laid off and be able to collect unemployment as I write!

Nick's Day
Getting Stuck Up on the Way to Work

© 2016 James LaFond

Saint Patrick's Day, 3/17/16

A former black coworker of mine was leaving for work yesterday morning, turning the corner from Penn onto North Avenue at 10 a.m. on a sunny early spring day, on a primary street shared with the Northeast District Courthouse, when a younger, innocent, unarmed, black man, wearing a ski-cap on this 80 degree day, pulled it down over his face into a ski-mask, came face-to-face with him on the sidewalk, presented a gun from a close draw [holding the bent elbow of his gun hand close to his ribs] pointed at Nick's belly, and said, "Empty yo pockets, yo."

Nick turned out his pockets, which contained his keys, a stick of gum, his cell phone, and one dollar and twenty seven cents he had pocketed to buy a soda at work.

He was then told, with a wave of the handgun [an automatic of a type he could not identify, which seemed kind of small to him], "Walk on, yo—git up da way."

As he resumed his walk to work, an effort that would not cover the replacement of the phone, his keys rattled down the sidewalk behind him, so he turned tentatively and picked them up as the robber jogged away down the sidewalk.

Nick made it to work on time and his manager bought him a soda.

Nick's day was a typical day in the life of a working black man living among black criminals, a secret life with no meaning, for Nick's terrorized life does not matter, unless, of course, it is taken by a white man. But since Nick is a working man, and gives himself precious few opportunities to fight police officers and does not attack white men, it is very unlikely that he will ever matter in Urban Plantation America.

'Going Out with A Gun'
An Interview with a Retired Baltimore County Cop

© 2016 James LaFond

Okay, this was a while back, back in the day. I was stationed in the Essex Precinct. Now, over in Cockeysville, you get a call, and go to sort it out, you control the situation by saying, "Sir, please, sir, step aside while I do my job," and the situation is soon resolved.

Most of my beat was black apartment complexes. But mostly, they stole shit, robbed people and shot each other. They would run from a cop. Today it's a different story, like this guy back in December in Towson. He was told three times by police to leave these people alone and he kept coming back challenging the cops. Now he has to be cuffed. But if the guy is fighting you, you need to knock him on the head a bit so the hands come loose and you can cuff him—and the politicians are all over it. Shit, back in the day, the blackjack would have come out on that joker. The point is, nowadays the black dudes—a certain set of them—think they're tough, but aren't and try to fight you like the tough white dudes from the docks and Sparrows Point used to do. But these guys are pussies and are immediately crying injury and suing, where, back in the day, the Polish muscle head would have been, "Oh, well, you got me this time, but it took three of you!"

Anyways, back in the day, in Essex, it was mostly drunk white domestic calls. If the old lady was not messed up too bad, you could leave if she said she was okay. Of course you don't tell him that. Once I get the call for a domestic I have to go in. But nine times out of ten you've got some tough muscle guy in a wife-beater standing at the door drunk telling you everything is okay. I'm like, "Look, pal, this is going to go one of two ways, I talk to her and leave, or you don't let me talk to her and you leave with me."

Now you have to get through the door and it might happen right there, fighting some dude in his doorway.

This one time I get this call and this big, lean, tattooed biker guy is standing out front, won't let me in. He's saying, "Brother, this is my house and your ass is not coming in. Get the fuck lost!"

Then I see over his shoulder that the old lady—hiding back in the shadows—has two black eyes. Well, today, if she's got so much as a tear stain—he gets cuffed. But back in the day, brother, you just had to not bust her up. If she looks like that—like this little woman looked— you've got to go in.

Now, I know it's on and I have back up on the way when he takes a swing at me and I duck, trying to get behind him to cuff him, and he's switch-stepping back trying to re-cock for another swing and accidentally elbows me in the temple. He was just trying to keep me from getting behind him and disaster! Brother, I was in a bad way— could feel myself going out, dizzy, falling. Something he didn't even intend and I'm going out—felt like Alexis Arguello getting floored by Aaron Pryor.

But I cannot go out.

I have a gun on my hip.

If I go out, I'm dead, she's dead, and my backup is not walking into a fistfight but into a gunfight. It's not an option. You have to keep pushing.

Eventually I tripped him up and ended up on top and got the cuffs on him—how I don't know—but it's just gotta be. You can't go out when you're wearing a gun. Of course, regular people have no idea and these politically correct types, I suppose they want to get us killed in the line of duty and will come for you every time— guaranteed. I'm so glad I'm not a cop now.

-Jack

'At A Car Dealership'
A Jamaican among Irate Whites

© 2016 James LaFond

Once, when I was working at a car dealership in Pikesville, my boss changed the price on this car and an irate customer, a tough, Irish-looking guy—you know, one of those white people that don't give a shit—took offense to it.

So, I'm hanging round in case it gets physical. I always regard it as an employee's duty to make sure his boss doesn't get his ass kicked on the job. Then, and this was the last thing I would have suspected at the time—not yet being educated as to the various hatreds whites hold for one another—the encounter becomes racial!

I'm like, 'interracial shit between whites, this is new to me.'

The Irish guy keeps saying, "You're not going to Jew me out of my money you motherfucker."

Then, in his own defense, as if he were a black minister pulling out the race card, my boss said, "You know, I find your words to be insulting. I am Jewish, you know."

Then the Irish guys says, "Of course you're Jewish you Jew motherfucker, that's why your Jewing me!"

You know, once a person takes a hateful stance like that, there's not a lot of room for negotiation. My boss backed off the price and nothing got physical.

-Oliver

'Forty Acres and A Mule'
At Register #3 with the Ghetto Grocer

© 2016 James LaFond

Her name is Jenny, a tough chick of some forty years and of Polish descent. As I approached her register at the grocery dive I once worked for, I noticed her face was red and tear-streaked. I asked her if Mark [my former co-manager] was being mean to her, and she burst in a searing hiss of tears that vaporized before they flowed, emerging as steamy words, "It's only nine a.m. and I've already had one black man threaten me for not giving him a discount, talking about some kind of reparation bullshit. If that motherfucker wants some repairs, I' told him I'd knock those crooked teeth down his throat and he could get Obama to pay for his dentures."

As Jenny rang up my order, I offered some historical context, "During the Civil War, some union generals and politicians offered the slaves of their Confederate enemies title to the land they had been forced to work as a form of repair of the social contract, hence the term reparations, which a nation tat loses a war often pays to the victor, not unlike court-ordered restitution today. That never happened and they became wage slaves instead."

"Oh, you mean the same shit that's happened to me, loosing my house and renting on room on nine dollars an hour because some rich motherfucker lied to me and I believed it like some dumb Pollack?"

"Sure, it was a rich man's scam to get help from the poor against his rich enemies. It's the root of the term 'forty acres and a mule,' which has since come down to us as a metaphor for an un-fulfilled government promise."

Jenny slung my bag of discount pesto tortellini over to me as I handed her the ten dollar bill and she declared, "They got their forty acres on their independence card and I'm their goddamn mule—me and every poor bitch and bastard slaving away to feed their fat asses."

Throwing Larry Under the Bus
Picking Sides when Managerial Excrement Rolls Downhill

© 2016 James LaFond

"Throwing someone under the bus" is a perennial term among Harm City grocers, denoting the fine art of deferring blame to anyone other than yourself.

I once had an assistant manager who called me "The Senator," a black nerd who hated black men and women and could not wrap his head around the fact that I did not fire them at every opportunity. The employees named him "Erkle," which I think was the name of a similarly bispeckled, bow-tie wearing, big-headed, skinny black dude on some TV show. One thing was certain about Erkle, was that whenever he said to or about an employee, "Not meaning to thrown anybody under the bus—but..." then you absolutely knew that some poor clerk was getting tossed under the bus.

When Your Job Sucks

Many times I have had the pleasure of throwing a department manager or store manager, who towered above me in the hierarchy, to the not so tender mercies of the bus driver named Fate, whose avatar was generally a district manager. But Larry, I never wanted to throw Larry under the bus. The guy has hired me on two separate occasions and is one of the kindest, hardest working fellows I know. He feeds stray cats, reads science-fiction adventures, and has actually had the courage to mention the name of Donald Trump in a positive context around rabid democrats. John, Larry's boss, has also done me a few good turns. Of course, like any long time store manger, he can be a prick. Although, I have proudly noted that he's not half the dickhead I was when I was in his impracticable shoes. John walked up to me on a Tuesday morning after I had had an extended weekend, which was how I was spending my vacations, a little at a time, and said, "How was your weekend, sir?"

"Fine, John."

Then, pretending as if a grunt who makes $150 bucks a week can afford to travel and enjoy a jaunt to Atlantic

City—which is a Baltimorean's idea of a weekend getaway—he said, "So where did you go?"

"Nowhere."

He then turned to Larry, who was standing three feet away stocking the butter as I rotated the yogurt, and said, "Ask him to work this Saturday night."

As Larry began the obligatory, "I know your free time is important to you and that you spend it all writing," I was already laughing sardonically.

On numerous occasions Larry has tried to defend me from John's instinct to overwork a dropout from his managerial cult. I understand and appreciate them both.

Well, a few weeks ago, I was writing the fill order for the cottage cheese and sour cream section, as John and Larry argued over whose fault it was that there was no sign on the cream cheese display I had so aggressively featured in the bin. In reality, getting a sign on the shelf for a sales item is the grocery business equivalent of emergency dentistry in Bangladesh. The few people who can be trusted actually making price changes on the company software—this is in every retail food operation

I've ever worked—immediately develop a gatekeeper complex. They are the head of a two-person department that holds the other 7 departments hostage. Essentially, Larry and John were arguing over which one of them should have been trying to convince the scanning coordinator to do her job:

John: "How long has this Best Yet cream cheese been without a sign?"

Larry: "I don't know. Come on, you know the deal."

John: "This has been without a sign for three days!"

Larry: "I don't want to hear it, John. It's been two days at most."

John: "Jim, how long has this cream cheese been without a sign?"

Jim: "Since I built the display 14 days ago. I just assumed you guys didn't want to sell it."

John: "Get a sign, Larry!"

Larry: "Thanks a lot, Jim. You couldn't have shaved off a week, not even a day? Ah, it's okay. I haven't been under the bus for three days—was beginning to miss the smell down here!"

There you go, another minute in the life of a ghetto grocer, an occupation in which the man without humor is without hope.

'Because I'm Black!'
Thrown Under the Bus on Saturday

© 2016 James LaFond

Larry—the grocery manager I occasionally toss under the bus—asked me how things were this morning, and apologized for forgetting to order something for my section after he gave me an extra day off this weekend.

"I really am sorry. But I was so stressed. The owner is on vacation so the other managers all skated and left me holding the bag. Come on! Saturday is the busiest day of the week and the management team is almost entirely absent? That's going to change when Mister C. gets back. I tried to keep it together but the front end was just insane. It's hard to remember to cross all of the Ts and dot all of the Is when the world goes to Hell.

"It was Saturday afternoon and I was paged upfront because a man was threatening a cashier. Surprise—he was black. He had come in with a white guy and when he began screaming obscenities at the lottery machines one of the cashiers [a white woman] asked him to stop because there were children around. He then goes after her, screaming about racism and keeping a black man down. Now, his friend did interpose himself between the raging idiot and the woman. By the time I get up there he has been ranting and raging and threatening for minutes. I'm a little old white guy and he's a big young black guy. How is this going to play out? I'm no fighter. I simply asked him if he could stop screaming, hoping that he wouldn't haul off and floor me and he began screaming about me picking on him for being black, 'Oh, you're racist—this is all because I'm Black!.

I suppose I was not respecting his dialect—was suppressing his cultural expression.

I could not even get in a word in edgewise and had no way of resolving the situation, so I called someone that could and they were here in one minute. I was impressed with the Baltimore County Police Department. When the cops rolled he was singing a different tune, calmed down and claimed it was all a misunderstanding. How did you ever survive at Bel Garden? The last time I was there I did not see a single face of European descent. Why do they act like this?

I answered, "Their mothers use them as a meal ticket and beat the shit out of them—full on face punches in public from age three—and then use all of the EBT cash and food stamps to feed their boyfriends, except for the all meat hotdogs and ramen noodles they throw at the kids, who begin cooking at around five. When the kid morphs into a youth and nears adulthood, he will no longer bring in money—unless she was lucky enough to have lived in a unit with peeling lead paint and she can sue for his brain damage. So, she trains him to argue and rage at authority figures in hopes that he gets maimed or killed by the cops or some white guy defending himself, and then sues for all she is worth. There are lawyers that specialize in making windfall cases for welfare mammas whose abused boys become statistics.

Freddie Gray basically gave his life so his mamma could get a new house and SUV."

Larry responded, "Thanks, now I'm absolutely certain that I woke up in Hell this morning."

I did give Larry and his two assistants a briefing on how to diffuse such situations non-violently, which will be featured as an article, soon.

The Janitor and the Madman
A Phone Call from Jaylene: 6:07 a.m., 6/14/2016

Jaylene was a good worker. She also thought I was a good boss and is among the handful of my former employees who, some six years after my resignation, still call me for advice on dealing with their current manager. So, at six this morning, while working Mister John's yogurt case in Harm County, I receive a call from Jaylene, at Cheapskates Are Us in Harm City.

"Mister Jimmy, I got some shit to tell and wonderin' how to compose it so Mister Mike don' flip the fuck out!"

"Okay, Jaylene what is the matter."

"Mister Jimmy, I got me this nasty somebody on da night crew who sneak back to the men's room while I'm picking up the carpets up front—I know it—I seen his nasty ass creepin' on back to do his business! Mister Jimmy, this bitch is about to fuck a nigga up! I'm gonna go the fuck off!"

"No you're not, Jaylene. You're a professional. Take a breath. You good?"

"I'm good, Mister Jimmy."

"So, what is the problem—not who, but what?"

"Okay, Mister Jimmy, you know how you got your nasty so-in-sos dat spray and just up en leave. Nasty as it is a spray bottle makes quick work a dat shit—but I done got myself a worser problem den dat—the Mad Shitter, I call him, is a nasty ass!"

"Jay—"

"I'm sorry, Mister Jimmy, but a nigga done drop some shit like dat on your morning en you'd be fixin' ta whoop dat ass your own self! Fifth day in a row dis shit has happened en I'm fed up. Da firs time I thought some crackhead had an abortion—look like a fetus—what kina muvafucka eat a loaf a bread en it come out, still a loaf a bread? How is dat shit even humanly possible? You know, Darnay said he be watchin' dat porn en the human ass—"

"Jaylene!"

[Silence.]

'"What do you need from me?"

"Well, dat shit is so ridiculous—I mean I don't need to be standin' in front a Mister Mike explainin' dis shit—en I sho as shit don't need to be breakin' dat shit up with the dustpan—the plunger wasn't gettin' it. So I fixed a dustpan up on da end of a mop handle with some duct tape—well, like I said, I'm sick a dis shit, so I took a picture and was goin' ta email dat shit ta Mister Mike— or you think I should email it to you first?"

"Raylene, the picture in my head is going to take long enough to erase. I don't need one on my phone. And as far as Mike goes, you know the only time he has to check his emails is while he's eating lunch, right?"

"Oooooooh, Mister Jimmy, you so smart. So what do I do about dis shit?"

"Speak to the mad man, politely, as a janitor—as a professional. Explain to him your technique for taking care of the problem, demonstrate it even. The thing about being a professional, Jaylene, is to take care of things at your level. Okay?"

"Oh, thank you so much, Mister Jimmy. You have a blessed day."

A Freudian Typo
A Reader Sent in a Typo from an Employment Application He Was Filling Out

On a Government Job Application:

"Chief Officer of Human Capital"

And a BT-1000 grammatical challenge

"Bilangual in Spanish is a Preferable"

Another ridiculous typo, but amusingly apt

"US Citizen or Greed Card Required"

When You Suck!
And Your Job is Actually Much Better than You Deserve

Yesterday Tony was laid off.

Upon hearing this news from Nadia about her brother I gave my condolences, and then she filled me in on the rest.

Three months ago Tony was driving the supply truck for his boss's construction company, who pays him $20 per an hour to get the $15 per hour Mexicans back and forth to the job site with their gear.

Unfortunately, through no fault of his own, on his way to work, while drinking vodka and orange juice, smoking pot and eating Oxys, Tony discovered that this light pole just popped up—like bam!—right in the middle of the hood and Mexicans and tools and boards and nails and tortilla chips and shit were flying all over the place.

The responding Baltimore County Police officers did not test Tony to see if he was drunk—because he fucking rolls stone cold like that and they had no idea. They did, however, find his Oxys and his pot, so those useless, do-gooding rednecks locked him up. Tony spent a month in jail until his boss bailed him out, rehired him, paid his fine, gave him a new truck—and brand new Mexicans too—and sent him back out on the road. It's house building season, bro!

Well, every week for the last two months, Tony's boss has been reminding him that he had a piss test coming up this past Thursday. Hell, Tony had more piss test warnings then a UFC heavyweight contender!

Tony didn't show up for his piss test on Thursday, so his boss laid him off.

Oh well, I suppose that someone else will have to paint the curb with fresh Mexican...

Mamma Cake
When Your Job Sucks at the Artistic Level

© 2016 James LaFond

Yesterday, Larry, my long-suffering and beleaguered boss, was filling in for his boss, running the store, when a notorious cake customer came in with a complaint and a demand for a price reduction on the cake she ordered. It is common, for welfare mothers and grandmothers to buy at least one large, decorated cake per month with their food stamps [EBT food, these days]. The decorated cakes are either topped with icing printed photos of loved ones or decorated according to catalogued patterns for iconic pop culture figures, like R2-D2, CP3O, Oprah, etc. This lady targets the newest cake decorator and places an order for something outside the catalogue, in this case Yoda—the green humanoid Jedi of douche bag legendry—knowing full well that the young lady will not be able to replicate the image by hand without a pattern. She then complains, tries to get the employee fired or disciplined, and demands a 50-80% discount.

I thought Larry parried Mamma Cake's charge of poor customer service well:

"You know, this is not in the catalogue and you did not even speak to our top cake decorators to find out if it was possible, but went to a new girl. Now, we can stand here and look across that counter all day, and we will not see Michael Angelo, Leonardo Di Vinci or even Goya, pass behind the counter to take up an icing tube. If you want professional art, done freestyle from a picture, go to Woodlea Bakery, and they'll make you a cake with Yoda's face on it for a hundred and fifty dollars. I realize I am in charge, but I can't paint this image with icing any more than you can, and I cannot demand art from a bakery clerk."

Yes, when your job truly sucks and you are lucky enough to be a grocery store manager, you have numerous such opportunities to discuss the meaning of subsidized life with the soulless savages that exist in that matrix, that pinnacle of human achievement towards which all of the labors of the ancients and the scientists of the modern age propelled us, into an age when fools who believe themselves to be free are taxed to pay for the venal gluttony of beasts more vile than any horror that crawled forth from a Mesozoic swamp.

'Welcome Back, Larry'
When Your Job Sucks so Bad it Drives You to Contemplate Infinity!

© 2016 James LaFond

Forty-Four years on the grocer job and three years before retirement, Larry's job truly sucks. There is one perk, though, four vacation weeks per year, one for each complete decade served in the retail food trenches, lifting, moving and displaying countless carbohydrate delivery systems as the guy in the tie asks you stupid questions and makes useless suggestions, and the douche bags in the aprons fail you at every turn on the polyhydron of inventory control. Then there are the old ladies ramming your shins with the shopping cart bumper to get your attention, the sex-crazed, bi-polar, middle-aged broads trying to feel you up in the aisle, the mud sharks with their teaming food stamp-bred broods—the 300 pound shoplifters who tuck the ham shank under their arm and relive their Jim Browne fantasy with you as the stand-in for the undersized Caucasian corner back circa 1965...

Last Monday morning, at about 8:00, as Larry corrected the chip vendor's order, corrected George's faulty rotation and fretted over Big Ed's shitty merchandizing, he took a phone call, which at least permitted him to make faces at the unseen customer, where, if the complaint had been made in person, he would be professionally bound to smile and nod agreeably to the middle-aged sounding man on the phone.

FB: "May I speak with the manager, please!"

Larry: "He is on vacation and will not be back until next week, sir. But if you need help now, I am filling in."

FB: "Yes, I was shopping in your store yesterday and had to have a bowel movement."

Larry: [Throws his coffee in the trash can and grits his teeth.]

FB: "Well, I have never used a men's room in any other supermarket with toilets so low-to-the-ground. Don't you think it is odd that you have the only low-to-the-ground toilets in Baltimore?"

Larry: "No, sir, I had no idea. In fact, I have yet to conduct a survey of Baltimore Area toilets in super markets."

FB: "Well, I will have you know, that not only are your toilets too low-to-the-ground, but you have no handicapped bar! How is person supposed to clean themselves properly with no handicapped bar?"

Larry: [Thought, "Really, really—this is how my first day back from vacation is going to play out?]

FB: "I would really appreciate it if you installed a handicapped bar. In fact, I may call OSHA."

Larry: [Thought, "Not an occupational issue!]

FB: "But the greatest affront is the low commode. A man should not have to sit in humiliation, in a public restroom, waiting for a person to enter so that he can plead for aid, and then have –some guy!—haul him off of the toilet seat!"

Larry: "I am so sorry, sir, that you restroom experience was substandard. I will forward your complaint to the manager and push for the handicapped bar—which really is an excellent suggestion. As to the dimensions of your preferred toilet seat, I will refer you to Mister John, who will handle this issue with all of the attention it deserves as soon as he's back from his vacation."

FB: "I really do wish you would stress the importance of accessible toilet seats to your boss. You have no idea how humiliating this is."

Larry: [Thought to self, "Exactly, because I'm not a Fat Bastard with nothing better to do with my time than test-fire supermarket toilets!"]

Larry: "I will do my best, sir, and thank you very much for sh-sh—opping with Box and Save."

Sometimes God is straight with us, and lets us know, in no uncertain terms, exactly where we stand or otherwise position ourselves.

I'm rooting for your, Larry, only 144 more Monday mornings to go!

Little Debbie's Big Idea
Dealing with Little Dindu Bitches or Dindettes

© 2016 James LaFond

I stopped at the Ghetto Mart for coconut water today and saw a sight.

Little Debbie is a big chick of Swedish descent who works as a cashier at a ghetto supermarket in Harm City, Maryland. She noticed that the lady who she had just checked out—a small, Dindu bitch in cut off jeans, wife beater and flip-flops with her hair woven with fake braids—had a box of fried chicken hidden under her shopping cart. She pointed to the security guard, who stopped the woman and asked her to pay for the chicken.

The little, 18-year-old-looking Dindette then began screaming, and swearing at Debbie, told her she wanted a refund, that it was Debbie's fault for not seeing the chicken, and that she was "from Wess Balmore, bitch," en we can take dis shit outside, where I'll whoop yo white ass—bitch!"

Debbie stepped out from behind the register and said, "Let's go, Bitch. I'll grab that wiglett of yours and scrub the sidewalk with your face!"

The Dindette, looking up at the husky paleface broad, then seemed to think better of her challenge, set the box of unpaid chicken on the register back, and left, looking over her shoulder nervously.

I love shopping at the Ghetto Mart.

'Death Tear Dude'
When Your Job Sucks and is Still Far Better than Your Customer

© 2016 James LaFond

Three weeks ago, on a Friday night/Saturday morning shift at about 2:30 a.m. Debbie, a stiff upper lip middle aged chick with three jobs was showing Alvin, the 18-

year-old new hire, how to check the roll rack in the bakery section to my back, as I broke down the dairy order.

The coffee pot is also one of the bakery floor clerk's details. A new pot was brewing, scheduled for the coffee bar self-serve counter at 2:45.

In struts the Death Tear Dude, ominously drunk, tattooed with three tears for each of the other thugs he has supposedly offed—old enough, at 50, to maybe not be bullshitting this point with the faded ink—lean, mean and in need of caffeine.

Finding the coffee thick and barely warm, he is feeling belligerent, t but is a nice drunk and decided to mix up his ominous posing routine with some friendly intimidation.

He looks at to complain and eye eye-fuck him, after months of getting beaten up by my young fighters in the mode to flex my white back hair in the masters division. I am usually super meek at work, but when assholes are prepared to get loud with non-combatant staff I ease into quite asshole mode.

When Your Job Sucks

He looks at Debbie and begins to complain and she fixes him with that—if you were my old man and were out this drunk this late I'd be waiting on the porch with a bat—stare of matriarchal disdain and snips, "Just add hot water, pointing at the hot water tap used for tea and hot chocolate."

St back on his Puerto Rican heels, the guy begins eye-balling Alvin and making gang signs, calling him brother, even "holmes," offering to be friends if the young dude is cool and respects his street cred and talking like Al Paccino, as fictional Cuban mobster, imitating a South Baltimore whigger, imitating a west Baltimore thug…

The kid tried to help Death Tear Dude as Debbie watched them and I watched him, and the guy eventually staggers away without his coffee mumbling, leaving behind a pretty well shaken sissy. You have to understand, that 18 is the new 12 in white suburban America and this Latino thug was pretty intimidating. The only reason I was confident in the event of physical exchange was his extreme drunkenness.

So, I looked the kid and said, "Alvin yo handled that quite well. That's Tucco, our new hire vetting agent.

John buys him a fifth of Baracrdi and a pack of tiparillos to give new guys a hard time to see if their management material."

The kid actually believed me for a second until Debbie patted him on the shoulder and smiled, to which laughed well, humor being the saving grace of the wage slave when his job sucks and the customers are worse!

'On Pay Day'
This Could Be Your Boss!

© 2016 James LaFond

"Old link is dead. Here's that Chinaman in Katanga. Zero fucks given:"

-U.K. Correspondent

I was waiting for that big-headed Negro to beat the shit out of this Chinaman.

No luck.

But still, what prick this guy must be to work for.

https://www.youtube.com/watch?v=6uqMh_q_HXI

'Bitches and Faggots'
The Mescaline Feed Locates a Long Lost Ghetto Grocer Employee

© 2016 James LaFond

"My God, they look like they live in an armory! Those are the same fences we saw at the Marine reserve depot."

http://www.dailystormer.com/another-black-kills-another-korean-war-vet/

"The chick in the video below is brassy as hell—I like how she starts getting on the men, calling them bitches and faggots!"

-Mescaline Franklin

Mescaline, the first item above has become so commonplace I wonder if perhaps U.S. war vets are being targeted by Government hate bots programmed to kill witnesses to evidence that the United States has actually employed soldiers to shoot at non-whites.

Okay, Bro, thanks for finally helping me locate Urethea, who was a pretty good seafood clerk until she started screaming to a cringing gentle giant who had criticized the length of time it took her to steam his shrimp, "Well you big baby bitch, you can suck my dick!" came the scream heard round the store—Ghetto Grocer to the customer rescue, with ill-fitting tie, bent glasses and clipboard of disciplinary forms....

I took Yereatha into the meat room [behind the seafood counter] in order to inform her that she had been politically incorrect, and immediately became concerned that she might have been anatomically correct in her outburst and kept my distance as she gushed tears of anger, paced, pirouetted while biting her lips angrily, wrung her hands and reached out to me for an understanding white daddy hug as I scanned the room for knives and thankfully found none laying about. In submitting to the hug, under the condition that I got the over-hook position and she took the pummel position, I was relieved to have felt no prodding bulge [hopefully indicating that she was bluffing] and that her breastessez were not phony or of the bitch-tit variety, but actual female—if undersized for her ethnicity— organs. I managed to get her calmed down enough to relieve the deli clerk who had stepped into the breach and made certain to hover around the counter merchandizing breading and spices in case another negro criticized her steaming time.

Unfortunately, Yereatha failed to return to work the next day and I never saw her again. So thank you, Mescaline, for sending evidence that she seems to be gainfully employed somewhere in Urban America and has lost none of her infamous pluck.

The Ghetto Gourmet

The Ghetto Gourmet
The $15 Grocery Budget, or How to Survive Selling 300 Books A Year

© 2015 James LaFond

Once again today, at the dojo, and at the Peruvian chicken joint where I opted for the cheapest item on the menu—which my son's friend understood as some ancient form of self-sacrifice echoing down through the ages from some unthinkably stark pit of want—I was met with astonishment when admitting to the infamous $15 a week grocery bill.

$15 was my starting food budget when I moved into this elevated man cave—some might say returned whence my arboreal ancestors came. That money was not required. As soon as my sister, the women at work, the mothers at the karate school—and the lonely lady up the street—discovered that some literate and unattached human male was living such a Spartan existence I was swamped with more food than could fit into this tiny refrigerator. Soon my greatest problem was keeping the empty microwavable containers organized by woman. Gone were my austere dreams of rediscovering the six-pack protected by my flesh keg. Hell, the mother of one of my fighters drove by the house with the intention of winging a chicken sub up on the porch like a paper delivery driver.

Even when one tries to starve in this food-saturated world avoiding the avalanche of food is impossible. Now my estate manager has acquired a woman who likes to cook in large quantities and is ever bringing the tasty bowl of this or that to my austere door.

As it stands I spend $15 per week on groceries, most of which I consume on my coffee break and lunch break at work, only carting home about $5 worth of food per week.

I budget $20 a week on dining out. With a single folding metal chair and a 10 by 14 inch tray table, I am not exactly set up for entertaining. I also spend about $20 a month on drinking out, which essentially means that renting a room for $400 costs me an additional $100 per month to socialize away from it.

So really, when speaking of my active grocery budget, we are looking at one bag of groceries that have cost about $5: beans, peas, noodles, shredded wheat, deli-cheese-ends, etc. This haul nets me three 'writer-made' meals per week, and various celebratory dishes enjoyed with 2 cheap beers in the wake of a just finished book—the twice monthly not-even-close-to-starving-author's triumph.

The Ghetto Gourmet will be devoted to such delicacies. I was going to describe the meal that shall not be eaten because I have gotten accidentally drunk [back to that later]. Instead I shall promote the Irish writer's favorite past time, with a Harm City twist.

The Roaring 40

My liquor of choice is rum—as I fancied myself a pirate as a boy, until I discovered I'd have to be a homo. My Rum of choice is—was—Myers. I have bracketed down from Barbados rum, to Jamaican rum, and finally to Puerto Rican rum, and have settled for Castile, which can be gotten in a glass bottle—very important—for 6.99 for 7.50 ml at the fine liquor emporium out in Harm County where my son purchases his Mount Gay rum for $30.

That was a good deal, the single bottle being used medicinally to relieve cramps twice, thrice to help me get to sleep for my 3 hour nap before work, and finally fueling a sorry little excuse for a party.

Not a bad deal. Rather than pick up the weekly six pack of $4.59 beer and hazard those bubbles before bed, I decided to head down to John's Korean liquor store for a bottle of Castile—and it was $18! It was Wednesday and I had but $15 to my name. Then I saw it there, on the bottom shelf:

Imported

Port Royal

40% alcohol (80 proof)

West Indies

Rum

Imported and bottled by Majestic Distilling Co., Inc., Baltimore, Maryland

This stuff has the aroma of paint thinner and tastes like the plastic bottle. No, it tastes much worse than plastic. The ship with the wind in its sails behind West Indies Rum does offer hope of –I suppose the same kind of roaring hangover enjoyed by actual pirates.

All is not lost. The taste can be improved to the point where you should be able to drink a shot straight without one of your eyes dropping out.

1. Transfer the contents of the nasty plastic bottle into a glass bottle. I prefer Everfresh glass pint and long neck 24 ounce bottles, which I use for bottling and chilling tap water.

2. Insert 1-3 slices of crystalized ginger and shake vigorously.

3. Place in the refrigerator and you will have something almost as smooth as the worst Puerto Rican Rum.

4. Mark the bottle! In this way you might avoid accidentally downing 4 shots in one gulp thinking that the clear liquid is water. I was supposed to be writing about something else just now but it has slipped my mind.

Enjoy, and do not eat the ginger once it has soaked in the rum. I warned you.

Food Stamp Soup
The Ghetto Gourmet Celebrates the End of Free Money with a $1.60 Feast

© 2015 James LaFond

To supplement my nickel an hour writing fortune, I stock the dairy case and frozen food section at Free Food For Fat ^%#@! twice, or even thrice, weekly. Between the 6th and the 16th those who choose not to work for a living, as well as working folks who have bought some dope fiend's baby's EBT food allotment for 50 cents on the dollar, flood into grocery stores to purchase animal flesh, sugar, sodium and bleached flour in all of their mind boggling configurations; such as Sunny Delight, an artificial juice made of water, hexametaphosphate, high fructose corn syrup and flavored with 'ester of wood resin,' which sells for more than the actual orange juice in the case next to it.

Obesity is on the rise and business is booming. So, when I finally worked my way out from under that truck load of kidney stone precursors and trudged home, I lacked the energy for intensive food preparation. Yet I wished to eat like a king, or the kind of king with his crown on his teeth and his pants down around his knees who normally revels in such fare...

I grabbed the $1 4.3 ounce Nissan Souper Meal, a collection of sixty ingredients including six types of sodium. That 4.3 ounces might not sound like much but it is dry weight. The cup holds a quart of water. Arriving home with my soup, soup pot, and soup bowl, all in one neat package with a picture of the stalwart cow that was horribly butchered to give up her powdered sinews to provide this primate with 14% of his USRDA of protein, I took stock of possible additional ingredients much like the old time soldier with the soup stone recruiting dining partners, resulting in the following process:

When Your Job Sucks

1. Crush the dry noodles lest they wiggle from your mouth and snake into your keyboard while you are proof reading what that failed boxer wrote yesterday.

2. Break open the packet of dehydrated vegetables and spread them around, with no great hope that the corn will fail to pass completely through you unchanged.

3. Do not neglect to spread the packet of desiccated beast essence and sodium compounds.

4. Dip into your coat pocket and dig out that old 50-cent fire cracker bar sausage you forgot to eat on Christmas Eve when Betty showed up with the hot wings. Slice it just so. For some extra tang pour the vinegar/red #4 dye solution in.

5. Those six packets of ketchup that your roommate left on the coffee table last week after he wolfed down his sub can turn this into a proper minestrone.

6. Two cloves of garlic, sliced fresh, should go on top as they tend to sink.

7. A handful of those wasabi peas will go a long way toward clearing those traumatized nasal passages, if you, like me, had your nose smashed in two days ago.

8. A teaspoon of madras curry powder or sliced ginger.

9. A squirt of hot sauce

10. Fill the cardboard bucket to the rim with 24 ounces of water and nuke it until it smells like day old fried rice. My little apartment food nuker takes 8 minutes, which is the frozen vegetable setting twice.

I have found this recipe quite tasty. However, eating it every day will probably turn you into something resembling the corn in the packet as one bowl has 112% of your daily sodium. I like this in the summer mostly, after I have perspired a great deal

Pre-date Warning: Dudes coming out of prison call this 'hook up' and are in the habit of adding tuna fish. Look, unless you want your room to smell like a West Virginia whore house in August, I suggest adding no tuna, especially if you have finally talked the barmaid into delivering your six pack.

Bottoms up.

The $2.50 Ghetto Publication Partay
How To Reasonably Celebrate the Completion of a Book Expected to Earn $10 in Royalties Per Year

© 2015 James LaFond

In **The Ghetto Gourmet** I described, under The Roaring 40 at the bottom of the page, how one could take nigh undrinkable cheap rum and make it bearable by the shot, primarily for medicinal purposes. But what about for sipping, when you want to get buzzed in a considered and meaningful way while enjoying a video diversion?

For The Ghetto Gourmet 'Partay Time' is post three o'clock on Friday, after I have proofed or published or finished a book.

Once, over a year ago, having qualified for my excuse to get drunk at my desk, I decided to review a movie instead, Black Dynamite **'Got Kung Fu Bitches'**. Immediately becoming enthralled by this blackxploitation spoof that somehow failed to win an Oscar, and without taking my eye off the screen, I reached behind me for the beer can slot in the door of my three-foot high apartment fridge, conveniently in reach of this seat. I grabbed the cold can and savored the hiss of released carbonation as Michael Jai White argued on the phone with his aunt about interrupting his 'Kong Fu' practice.

And what was the taste I put to me lips, but orange soda, left over from Latiffah's visit on the previous Saturday night. Having expected a National Boh aroma, I was stricken by the irony of holding a ghetto favorite in my hand while watching a movie about that 'diabolical motherfuca' Richard Nixon distributing 'dick shrinking' malt liquor among the black population. Reaching for the six dollar bottle of Port Royal rum, proudly bottled in Baltimore, I decided to pause the movie and cook up a proper partay platter.

Laffiffa had left all of the fixings for my feast. So, I mark the expense at 2.50 cents because I only went through 3 of the 12 condoms that came in the $10 box that I had purchased in celebration of her pending visit that previous Saturday night. All I need do was survey her remaining largesse, so thoughtfully left for my consumption, to work up a nice snack tray.

1. The used paper plate that she had thoughtfully neglected to place in the trash can—where some snobby bitch would have put it—but had instead left at the foot of the bed

2. The remains of her bottle of Texas Pete wing sauce

3. The unfinished bag of cheese curls, very important, as I was fresh out of cheese, as none had gone out of date and been reduced by Mister Mike down at the Ghetto Depot lately

4. The remains of her bag of Tostitoes tortilla chips

Preparation Instructions

1. Place the corn chips on the plate, layered like roof shingles

2. Squirt plenty of wing sauce on the chips

3. Crush the cheese curls into a fine powder and sprinkle on the chips, to which the powder will adhere due to the wing sauce

4. Use the remainder of the wing sauce to heavily douse the cheese curl powder, as this will hydrate the powder and turn it into an approximation of squeeze cheese—albeit on the hot side—while being nuked.

5. Slice a clove of raw garlic over the plate, so that when Mom calls you up to make sure you haven't eaten processed foods all week long, you don't have to lie when you tell her you had fresh vegetables for dinner.

6. Nuke that plate on the beverage setting.

Enjoy your plate of victuals with your store brand orange or grape soda mixed two parts two one with your ginger infused cheap rum, mixed in a wine glass—provided by my wine drinking son when he invested in a new cherry wood wine glass cabinet that deserved to house better wine glasses—to lend ambiance to the cinema experience.

Disclaimer

Don't try fixing this for Latiffah. Just hand over the carry out menu for the Pakistani Pizza Parlor and get some rest—you'll need it.

The Crack in the System
A Note on The Slave Master's Blind Spots

© 2015 James LaFond

Many who live today look with dread on the massive surveillance machine and debt slavery racket that seems forever expanding. Occasionally, though, I see signs of hope that these massive social systems—based as they are on central planning concepts—shall fail.

Today I spoke with a bookkeeper at a supermarket chain that has changed out the brand of coin-trading machines for the very centralist corporate thinking reason that the new contractor puts more information in the hands of the retailer in the form of scanned cash voucher receipts, as opposed to the old style coin receipt that I used to have to sign and physically forward for redemption.

There is just one small glitch: the receipt printer uses the very same paper as the registers, with the result that up to 30% of vouchers are discarded as trash by the overworked and under-motivated staff.

And there is no one that can be contacted about this at corporate because all information based transaction concerns are now routed through a help desk in India, whose switch board operators speak a dialect of English as alien to American English as possible. Only one employee has the patience to spend the half hour necessary waiting on hold, to spend the 1 hour necessary to get a sentence translated, to get closer to a technical solution. So, vouchers go uncashed, registers with programming issues remain idle, with the retailers of this and other chains beginning to show systemic cracks that might pop up in the machine manned by our Masters' Loyal Slaves.

When can hope.

Ghetto Pot Pie
A Rare 10 Minute Delicacy from the Ghetto Gourmet

© 2015 James LaFond

I came home to an empty refrigerator. But never fear, the Ghetto Gourmet is here.

I have a pyrex thing, kind of like a two inch deep glass pie plate, given to me by someone who does not want me ingesting any more estrogen mimicking chemicals from heating plastic plates. I clean this thing once a week, which gives some continuity to the flavor of my food, making Friday's supper kind of a medley of the week's menu—the dietary week in review you might say.

I do not buy bread as it gets smashed in my backpack, and making bread with this coffee pot and microwave has so far not worked out. As my only food stuffs were canned stews and soups left over from Mister Mike's last March clearance sale, and I'm a bread sopping kind of guy, I hit on a compromise. Instead of a 24 ounce can of Dinty Moore stew without bread to mop up the valuable micro-nutrients in the gravy before it solidifies back to its original solid state, I made a pot pie.

Ascend the carven stair.

Behold the realm of Anu and Ishtar.

Look beneath the corner stone.

Unlock the sacred box.

Gaze upon the tablets carved by that unpaid slave who got chucked in the irrigation canal after he...

Listen to the epic of Whitetrashgmish, of how he experienced all, suffered all, conquered—well, his dietary needs at least...

Okay, it's just a room with books laying all over the place and thoughtfully covered with clean clothes—well, really I pile the clothes on the books because the books are in front of the dresser.

Yes, the pot pie.

Smash 4 stale, generic taco shells into a fine aggregate and spread evenly on the bottom of the glass plate-bowl-thing with the proprietary name that is not in the Word 2007 dictionary.

Open the can of stew with the tab facing away and the can mouthing open towards you, because it is going to be easier to wash that shirt than it is going to be for me to wash that damned curtain with the girly weave that Tannika bought me.

Pour the stew out in the middle of the bowl-thing and try not to be discouraged by the plopping dog food sound, because it's going to taste pretty good.

The stew is really thick, so won't spread out and cover all the taco shells. If you try to spread it with your only spoon, then you will have to use another napkin, and they cost. So, to save your last plastic spoon from getting coated with cold grease, find the coffee filter on the old lady's dresser that used to live in this room an examine the contents. In this case I found six Taco Bell salsa packets and dripped them over the exposed taco shell crumbs around the congealed stew perimeter. But duck sauce, soy sauce, ketchup, mayo, will all do fine. It's about the moisture, about turning that lime treated cornmeal into mushy crust—and it worked.

I placed a paper plate over the top of the glass pie bucket and nuked it on dinner plate three times, hitting the beverage setting once for good measure, and "Bam!"

Thank You, Sean
The Ghetto Gourmet Gets an Upgrade

© 2015 James LaFond

Sean recently gave a sizable donation to:

"That Fellow's James LaFond,

Slumming in a Negroid Pond."

-The Red Skull

The generous donation came with the following stipulation:

"We'd like you around for a while, so you can pass on these arts before you kick the bucket. So please, no more ghetto pot pies. Buy yourself some decent food and live a little longer."

Thank you, Sean, and I will do so. Ishmael and Shayne are older than I am, and I'd feel terrible if they had to carry me down off some mountain next year.

Thus far I have purchased green tea bags, herbal tea bags, three pounds of oats and a pound of raisins, two bags of dried lentils, two bags of frozen mixed vegetables, two bags of split peas, and two bunches of garlic.

I added this order to my present larder of figs [a 12 once bag], two packs of all beef hotdogs that I bought and froze the day they went out of date for a reduced price, three cans of white tuna and a jar of peanut butter.

You can keep up with my delicious meal recipes as they come to aromatic fruition!

I have a microwave, a coffee pot, and a 2-quart crock pot stacked on top of my little refrigerator.

Thanks again, Sean

PS: I hope to be light enough to box [spar, not compete] by spring.

Sinus Soup
No, This is Not What Comes Out of Your Foe's Broken Nose

© 2016 James LaFond

For a guy who has been punched in the nose to the point where one nostril is pretty much closed and the other has a cyst up by the sinus cavity by the eye, I do what I can to keep these passages open.

I snort saline solution three times a day.

Once a day I snort Listerine during cold and flu season.

Below is the soup I make for clearing my sinuses.

I use a quart and a half crock pot, which fits next to the coffee pot on top of the microwave.

Ingredients

One clove of garlic, sliced

One teaspoon of horseradish

One teaspoon of curry or cayenne powder

One quart of beef broth had for sale at the ghetto grocer's for $1!

Directions

Heat it on high for three hours.

Put it down on low for an hour.

Grab some old socks with holes in them [Not the ones you used to clean the beer you spilled partying with Charmenique off the floor] to keep from burning your hands and dump it into something you can drink out of.

Mix it up with a spoon.

Down the hatch.

Two Ghetto Gourmet's In Action

Tommy Sotomayor: Black Waffle House Weave Heads Caught On Camera Doing Hair In The Kitchen Using Food Utensils!

© 2016 James LaFond

Last week I went to see a serious movie and sat along with the rest of the predominantly middle aged white suburban moviegoers. To our right was one black couple, a well dressed pair in their mid thirties. The sixth or seventh movie trailer was of a horror film. When a zombie leaped from off screen upon an actor the black woman screamed at the top of her lungs, as if old Nathan Bedford Forest hand caught her hanging William Tecumseh Sherman's laundry on his clothesline.

Far from being offended, the theater erupted into laughter, as the movie trailers had been positively dreadful and phony throughout, with this lady giving the best performance of the day until Leonardo Dicaprio took the stage.

I have viewed the following news story in the same entertainment-oriented vein. When a people—one of three of the five great races of Man that is not in imminent danger of extinction—declare universal lack of agency and seek succor at every turn from Asian and Caucasian, it is only fitting that their more personable members devote their energies to entertaining the rest of us as we all hurtle at the speed of blight toward extinction.

https://www.youtube.com/watch?v=-C3lumpynZI

Yomageddon
A Half Million Entitled Social Justice Heroes to be Martyred Today!

© 2016 James LaFond

"No joke: 500k food stamp recipients to lose benefits on April 1.

Just thought you should know. Batten down the hatches."

-Travolta

https://www.rt.com/usa/337926-americans-food-stamps-benefits/

Thanks, Bro. I know you are glad to be out of retail food for good.

From my reading of this the effect is going to be primarily on junkies and other lowlife forms, who will amp up shoplifting and panhandling and burglary. The welfare mammas and their vast broods will not be touched. The two populations of adults hit with this are going to be 20-something slackers and 50-something losers—mostly palefaces—the first group mostly addicts, the second group mostly being pushed out of the workplace by younger competition. The second group is mostly going to roll over and die and the first group is already causing trouble, so I think the result in supermarkets is going to be felt mostly by loss prevention operatives as an escalation of existing theft patterns and by the rest of us as more aggressive panhandling.

This will not be Yomaggedon, but a baby step toward eventual welfare-cutting measures that must eventually happen as the economy continues along its course, and will, in the end, spark more aggressive looting behavior. Do note that once looting occurs across a community, the looters discover how powerless the police are, and will continue looting activity at lower intensity indefinitely, which has happened in Baltimore, where much shoplifting is now indistinguishable from small scale looting.

Brain Juice
Reversing Big Sam's Recipe for Revelry

© 2016 James LaFond

Big Sam was a friend who would drink to face the world while awake, go to sleep when his blood threatened sobriety and then hit the coffee station hard at work in order to be productive enough to earn his booze money.

As a writer I have spent many a day struggling to stay awake at the keyboard. Without checking I cannot tell you what I wrote yesterday, or even how many articles I posted, but can verify that I woke up often while writing.

My stomach has lost the ability to handle coffee and I now require at least 2.5 hours of sleep to be able to get through a night of stocking yogurt and frozen pancakes without waking up in the case with Tia tapping me on the shoulder, "Mister Jimmy, you okay? You need me ta get Nokia ta swish on by in those clingy polyester pants?"

Once at work I drink one cup of half coffee/half cocoa.

Once at home in the morning I start the brain juice a brewing in an attempt to write as long as possible, with brain juice failure tending to hit between 3 and 10 p.m. As long as I am falling asleep gently and my head is not actually ponding I will keep drinking more brain juice and tapping away. But, after my second or third hard impact on the desk top or keyboard—the glasses look like they've been run over by a car—I turn on the nightmare-inducing Nordic ambient music or the serene Japanese Traditional YouTube feed and go to sleep.

The next morning, the brain juice gets cooking again. But, I need to have a cutoff point to reduce the brain juice in the blood or I have to reverse Big Sam's cure and blast the brain with alcohol [three beers does it] so that I can get to sleep. Today is such a day, so here is the brain juice procedure:

When Your Job Sucks

The out-of-work coffee put is used, with 12 cups of water in the upright tank.

In the bottom of the dry pot I place 2 English tea bags, 2 peppermint tea bags and a cinnamon stick.

Hanging from the rim into the nectarious precinct are two green tea bags and a standard tea bag, or, on tough days a gingko/ginseng tea bag.

If me stomach is feeling rough, I drop in a slice of ginger or another peppermint tea bag.

If I do not have to coach in the afternoon I begin adding camomille to the brew, then stop drinking it. If I miscalculate, beer to the rescue at bedtime.

At whichever point I decide to turn the pot off I will bottle some for iced tea, setting the bottled out to seal and later placing them in the beer cooler.

In hot weather I brew a pot and bottle it at dawn and drink the refrigerated tea I brewed the day before.

There you go, juice for the groggy brain.

Yes, and when I have no time to heat something in the nuker, I pour quick oats into a cup and pour the tea on top of that, and eat that for breakfast, which I am doing right...now.

Throwing Larry Under the Bus
Picking Sides when Managerial Excrement Rolls Downhill

© 2016 James LaFond

"Throwing someone under the bus" is a perennial term among Harm City grocers, denoting the fine art of deferring blame to anyone other than yourself.

I once had an assistant manager who called me "The Senator," a black nerd who hated black men and women and could not wrap his head around the fact that I did not fire them at every opportunity. The employees named him "Erkle," which I think was the name of a similarly bespeckled, bow-tie wearing, big-headed, skinny black dude on some TV show. One thing was certain about Erkle, was that whenever he said to or about an employee, "Not meaning to thrown anybody under the bus—but..." then you absolutely knew that some poor clerk was getting tossed under the bus.

Many times I have had the pleasure of throwing a department manager or store manager, who towered above me in the hierarchy, to the not so tender mercies of the bus driver named Fate, whose avatar was generally a district manager. But Larry, I never wanted to throw Larry under the bus. The guy has hired me on two separate occasions and is one of the kindest, hardest working fellows I know. He feeds stray cats, reads science-fiction adventures, and has actually had the courage to mention the name of Donald Trump in a positive context around rabid democrats. John, Larry's boss, has also done me a few good turns. Of course, like any long time store manager, he can be a prick. Although, I have proudly noted that he's not half the dickhead I was when I was in his impracticable shoes. John walked up to me on a Tuesday morning after I had had an extended weekend, which was how I was spending my vacations, a little at a time, and said, "How was your weekend, sir?"

"Fine, John."

Then, pretending as if a grunt who makes $150 bucks a week can afford to travel and enjoy a jaunt to Atlantic City—which is a Baltimorean's idea of a weekend getaway—he said, "So where did you go?"

"Nowhere."

He then turned to Larry, who was standing three feet away stocking the butter as I rotated the yogurt, and said, "Ask him to work this Saturday night."

As Larry began the obligatory, "I know your free time is important to you and that you spend it all writing," I was already laughing sardonically.

On numerous occasions Larry has tried to defend me from John's instinct to overwork a dropout from his managerial cult. I understand and appreciate them both.

Well, a few weeks ago, I was writing the fill order for the cottage cheese and sour cream section, as John and Larry argued over whose fault it was that there was no sign on the cream cheese display I had so aggressively featured in the bin. In reality, getting a sign on the shelf for a sales item is the grocery business equivalent of emergency dentistry in Bangladesh. The few people who can be trusted actually making price changes on the company software—this is in every retail food operation I've ever worked—immediately develop a gatekeeper complex. They are the head of a two-person department that holds the other 7 departments hostage. Essentially, Larry and John were arguing over which one of them should have been trying to convince the scanning coordinator to do her job:

John: "How long has this Best Yet cream cheese been without a sign?"

Larry: "I don't know. Come on, you know the deal."

John: "This has been without a sign for three days!"

Larry: "I don't want to hear it, John. It's been two days at most."

John: "Jim, how long has this cream cheese been without a sign?"

Jim: "Since I built the display 14 days ago. I just assumed you guys didn't want to sell it."

John: "Get a sign, Larry!"

Larry: "Thanks a lot, Jim. You couldn't have shaved off a week, not even a day? Ah, it's okay. I haven't been under the bus for three days—was beginning to miss the smell down here!"

There you go, another minute in the life of a ghetto grocer, an occupation in which the man without humor is without hope.

Harm City Chili
The Greaseless Method of Making Crockpot Chili in Your Only Room

© 2016 James LaFond

Last year I received a crockpot—which I was told was a fitting gift to a crackpot—so that I might avoid nuking everything and perhaps eat from without the can on occasion.

In April, when Mescaline Franklin was in town to finish Hemavore, we needed some man food as our vary-scarred minds collided in the [what is this experimental construct that you people think has a purpose?—sorry, getting off subject—man food...]

When Your Job Sucks

Suffice it to say that this is a small crockpot, that fits on top of my microwave, next to my coffee/tea pot, which sits atop my little refrigerator, an arm's reach from here—and I have no idea how I gained weight writing… The Liver-Eater would not approve as a hoodrat head—even a small one—would just not fit in this pot.

-Dump a 12 ounce bag of diced frozen onion in the pot with a few cloves of garlic. Do not forget to take the frozen onions and meat out of your backpack. You have already been on the bus for an hour and half genius— really, this can get nasty if you forget about it.

-Take one pound of ground pork or ground beef and put it on top of the onions.

-Cover with seasoning. I like Jamaican dry jerk herbs with smoked paprika.

-Turn it on high.

-After you can smell it, stir it up with your roommate's wooden soup spoon.

-After the room starts to smell a lot and you can't tell the meat from the vegetables when you stir, then notice how the grease separates, figure out how much chili powder it's going to take to soak that grease up—like when you put cat litter on motor oil—and dump that in and stir.

-Turn the pot down on low.

-When it starts to smell like something your mother would have yelled at your father for cooking, then look see. If there is any grease still floating, get out the stale taco shells that Babelicious Capri donated for your nutritious taco meal that never happened, or the Doritos that Shaynequa was munching on when she interrupted your taco meal prep-work and crush these suckers up and mix in. The grease will not survive.

-Crack open a can of beer and enjoy.

White Nationalist Culinary Endorsement

Mescaline said, while spooning chili from my coffee cup, "This is good, man—fucking food, Bro."

I stand validated as a chef.

Got Meat?
When Your Ghetto Gourmet Sets a Challenge on Your Table

© 2016 DL

Does your Ghetto Gourmet Sweetheart bring you unusual food items from his local hood store (and I meant hood, not food) which were almost a pilfer, they were so inexpensive, and don't know what to do with them? Chalk this up to his Neolithic hunting and providing instincts.

Do you also buy too much food on sale impulse because it seemed like a good idea at the time? That's your gathering instinct, putting away for the leaner months.

That's how I came home with 15 pounds of frozen Brussel sprouts for $15. Well, they're vegetables and we need those, right? What could go wrong with this culinary inspiration? Boredom, that's what. My first two pounds were nicely fixed with garlic, sun dried tomatoes, onions and some sea salt. They went down easily, so I was quite pleased and optimistic.

Third pound, devil took the sundried tomatoes and hell ate the sticky, fresh garlic. So I just sprinkled some garlic powder and salt, combined with some bacon drippings as a quick and dirty cover up for lack of inspiration. Yeah, we ate 'em.

Went through my freezer today. Damn, I have a lot of Brussel Sprouts left. Oh, ef me, I still have 12 pounds! Why do I do this to myself? Also came across a few pounds of frozen franks and sausages, procured by my thoughtful GG who braved the rats on his way to the hood store to make sure that I am not famished and maintain my pleasing proportions.

When Your Job Sucks

That's it, it's on between me and the Brussel sprouts. I thunked four pounds onto the counter for defrosting, along with their sausage friends, which I much rather would have grilled and eaten with mustard than contaminated with the vulgar Brussel sprouts. Necessity will be a mother, however, and I will overcome out of sheer desperation.

Eight hours later, they have been cooked in a large skillet, the outside leaves somewhat burnt because I was getting back at them for jumping into my cart and coming home with me. My GG's 10 oz. single serve spaghetti sauce will serve well as a light coating to mask the damage to the outer leaves. The sausage will plead the innocence of his Brussel sprout clients, because they didn't have the advantages they needed to grow into cabbages, and all will serve as witnesses to each other and swear I coerced them into my cart. So into the oven they'll go for tomorrow's dinner, sprinkled with parmesan—you see where I'm going with this... and my Neolith will suck it down like a nursing baby does his mother's milk.

Besides, he didn't really come over for the meal, anyway, did he? So it's not that hard to gain forgiveness, even cause him amnesia, for culinary sins. Just make sure you have some beer handy, and do not, under any conditions, confess to him. This can also be payback for those vile chili lime tortilla chips he crumbled feta onto and then gave you beer in lieu of water—you see where he went with that... and if he weren't that calculating, he wouldn't make a good hunter.

Also, nothing against beer, mind you—it makes for a great transcendent experience.

Oh, and one more thing—make sure you thank your hunter for whatever he drags in to the hearth, just as he thanks you for what may be a lame apparition of dinner. If you accepted the thanks, then keep your mouth shut when faced with certain culinary challenge. Besides, sometimes the pickings are as wonderful as soft corn tortillas and brie, which can become a warm burrito of melted brie and grape jam, redneck version of the French crepe, thank you very much.

This is DL, reporting from ground zero of my own mad life (I mean that Britishly).

'Survival Rum'
Ghetto Gourmet Training For Drinking Rye at Altitude with Mountain Men

© 2016 James LaFond

Ishmael sent me a donation while back with advice to get some good whiskey. He prefers rye. I understand that whiskey is more popular in the West because hauling beer on horseback would just be too much of a pain in the ass. I have found a vast discount liquor store where my affluent son shops, that has much lower liquor prices than my normal stops.

I do not like the idea of drinking spirits stored in plastic. If tap water can leach chemicals out of plastic bottles I suspect alcohol can too. Besides, everything tastes worse out of plastic and better out of glass.

For my whiskey purchase I wanted to go with the 1.75 liter rye for $40, but thought that I might want some rum for the hotter days, for sipping while I read Black Vulmea's Vengeance. Now, I hate Jack Daniels, like Maker's Mark, and like Hayes Parker almost as much. Plus it's less than half the price of JD with 5% more alcohol by volume. The big glass bottle with the jug handle cost $21 and I am assured by the stern illustration of Colonel Parker that the nectar of the Confederate Corn gods is made only in small batches and is 100% genuine, distilled in North Charleston, South Carolina.

Now, for the pirate juice. Since I actually sell a book a day now, and could technically afford to live in the gym locker room if I quit my night job, I'm feeling like somebody now and would like to enjoy my rum, rather than dread it as a shocking cure all. No longer do I settle for the 25-cents an ounce Port Royale rum, bottled in Baltimore.

Largo Bay Silver Rum [and to think that I had no idea that Princeton, Minnesota was situated amidst sugar cane fields until now!] is on sale for only $16.99 for the 1.75 glass, jug-handled bottle. I liked spiced rum but it has a lesser alcohol content and I'm trying to prep the liver for drinking with two guys who are conspiring to get me drunk so I'll eat some raw coyote liver. I am also looking to protect my stomach, so I shall use the same substances that have made my switch to tea from coffee beneficial to my coffee-sensitive digestion.

Note, I am a sissy who drinks his spirits cold from the freezer.

I am taking a 24 ounce glass bottle and placing in it the following:

-three pinkie-sized pieces of trimmed and split ginger root

-two cinnamon sticks

-three fresh peppermint leaves, from the garden of the commandant's daughter

Drown that with your 40% rum and it will be as spicy as the spiced and diluted rums that come in between 30-35%. The alcohol is what extracts the flavor, so when they add water to the spiced and flavored rums it's not as good as this.

Two such containers will last me sixth months at a few shots each per week and a monthly toast with my literary coconspirator, Mister Franklin.

'A Natty Boh'
Or 'One-Eyed Man': The Poor Tour Brew of Choice in Harm City, Maryland

© 2016 James LaFond

When I was a boy we children were permitted to drink beer only when there was a family crab feast. I understand this would be a crime today, but the long arm of the law does not extend to the grave and my mother can claim to have been forced to agree to this by my father. Each child could drink 4 ounces of beer from a glass, beer that was poured from a can. This beer was always National Bohemian. This company had a brewery in Baltimore among others around the country. It was a regional discount beer that has somehow survived the big three America beers and the microwbrewery movement. There was National Premium, which was slightly smoother, and has recently been brought back.

The beer has been brewed since 1885 and has been intimately involved with baseball, with two trademark slogans I used to hear from play by play announcers and a third that is not trademarked:

"From the Land of Pleasant Living"

"Oh what a beer!"

"Ain't the beer cold!" which is also the title of the book by that play by play announcer.

The beer was conceived in the context of the beer league baseball culture of the late 19th century.

It is a good beer on a hot day, has a better taste difference when cold than most beers, and has a strong hops aroma unlike mainstream American beers, but only a mild hops taste, which makes it refreshing. There is not enough flavor to interfere with food taste and is marketed side by side with snacks more than other brews.

White guys usually drink it out of a can and sometimes a bottle or glass.

Black guys generally prefer it out of a mug from the tap or from a 40 ounce bottle, although 24-ounce cans have recently been marketed to black patronized liquor stores.

When Your Job Sucks

The locals of both races call the beer Natty Boh, with some older white guys just asking for "a one-eyed man," taking note of the distinctive one-eyed mustachioed icon, who is dressed up as a MLB catcher on the can I am drinking from. The Utz potato chip company, out of Hanover PA, have even married their potato chip girl icon to the one-eyed man in advertising.

The price of Natty Boh ranges widely as it is regarded as an acceptable fall-back retro-brew by moneyed hipsters.

Single 12-ounce cans can be had at micro brew bars for 2.50

A 16-ounce mug from the tap of a sports bar is running at $1.50.

A 30-pack at a liquor stores generally runs $17.00 with the 12-pack for 8.99 to 10.99

In ghetto liquor stores the 12-pack runs 7.99 to 8.99,

The 24-ounce can 1.50

And the 40-ounce glass bottle 2.25-2.50

I always make my first beer or two a Natty Boh, and if I'm going to be at the bar longer, will move up to an IPA for my last drink.

At home, when knocking myself out for a short nap, I add one shot of whiskey to a glass mug poured from a 12-ounce can and call it a day. The whiskey knocks me out and the beer waked my up in 2.5 hours.

Defrosting Casserole
The Meal that Fueled the Feature Article, The Immoral Moat of Suburbia

© 2016 James LaFond

What does a broke-ass, old-ass dude prepare and eat while illuminating the motherslutter of all conspiracy theories?

I bought no groceries this week, or last, as I am letting my 28-inch high fridge defrost this coming Monday. It is critical, as so much ice has built up in what used to be a little box, I cannot extract the bottle of Makers Mark I put there and Mescaline Franklin is coming to town on Tuesday...

When Your Job Sucks

1 fresh jalapeno, picked up from the floor of my roommate's kitchen while I was filling my tea pot and she was throwing produce at him while impugning his character and indicated she'd rather me eat it than slice it up for his heartless ass—way to take one for the team, Bro.

1 giant clove of purple elephant garlic, because I've got a lot of writing to do and if Mrs. Bedwrecker shows up I don't want her staying for long and she hates the smell of garlic...

4 not-so-fresh hotdogs, sent home with me on Memorial Day by my sister, yet still seemingly impervious to age...

1/2 cup of out of date cream cheese, forgotten about since June

Slice all of the solid ingredients in a pyrex dish.

Cut open the cream cheese container with a box cutter, so extraction of the sticky substance is made easy and drop the white blob on the jalapeno slices,

When Your Job Sucks

Slide the dish into the microwave on top of the soon to be beer-ready fridge and nuke until you can smell the hotdogs.

Take it out—if you don't like the smell of the hotdogs—and sprinkle some adobo with smoked paprika on the dog slices.

Nuke again until you can smell the jalapenos.

No, don't eat the jalapeno stem, you lazy bitch—who put that in there anyhow?

Crush up a handful of whole wheat crackers over the still stable blob of cream cheese and stir it all up. Eat with the same spoon you stirred it with to cut down on dishwashing since you already dirtied your knife.

Now enjoy, which means shovel it in before it gets cold or I told you so.

Later—I really could use a shot of that Makers Mark to clear my throat...

Barbaricue
Eating Good on the Bottom of the Postmodern Food Chain

© 2016 James LaFond

I had $15 dollars left this morning to last me until Friday. With zero in the defrosted fridge, and full up on beer and whiskey, all I needed was some meat.

On the way out of work I checked the meat case. Fortunately Paul had pork chops in sale to try and take customers from the new outfit that opened up down the street. Now pork chops are good, but you have to stand over them, look at them flip them,—and this is bad enough on a stove top let alone on the hot plate of your coffee pot.

But, where pork cuts are on sale in a store that cuts its own meat, you have the trimmings, ground up and ready to cook on your one quart crock pot that sits next to your coffee pot like two faggots at a Democratic Party rally. There was a pack of ground pork for $1.29 per pound that came in at four pounds, which will fit in that pot.

When Your Job Sucks

As soon as I got into my room I dumped the meat in the pot, back the wrapper with Mescaline's empty beer cans and dropped it into the trash can I dragged to the curb. Mister Weirton, I know that is not recycling. I am, however, recycling the pig, which thoughtless vegans like yourself fail to do.

On top of the meat went my last two cloves of garlic, pressure skinned between the oft broken fingers of the typing paw.

There wasn't much left in the garlic powder bottle, so bam, in there.

Te chili powder bottle was also nearly done—I there.

The smoked paprika is new—a gift from a buxom Hungarian wench—glu-glump, a about a quarter of the bottle in there, the rest dumped in the adobo shaker.

Jamaican Jerk seasoning?

Hell yeah, if the Ricans can come to this party Oliver's people are invited too—about a handful.

That was it six-12 a.m. it's smelling right good about now.

I borrowed a ladle from the ancient kitchen downstairs, scraped the burnt meat off the rim and mixed it in to improve the paprika, and I'd say I'm two hours out from a hot meal.

When eating on $20 a week you grab cheep meat when you can as we don't want to cut into the 12$ a week beer budget.

Eating on $20 Per Week
A Ghetto Gourmet Update: Inflation even catches up with lowlife writers

© 2016 James LaFond

I have spent my $20 food allotment for the week at Mister Mike's store, just down the road in the ghetto:

$3.00 1 42-ounce canister of quick oats

$2.00 4 9-once packs of fresh Exotic Mushroom ravioli

$2.00 2 8-once wheels of Il de France Camembert Cheese

$1.09 1 18-pack of corn tortillas

$4.00 1 16-pack case of Tina's beef, bean and hot pepper burritos

$4.04 3 pounds of ground pork shoulder

$1.39 1 bunch of giant garlic

$1.09 10 cinnamon sticks [for bottling my own tea]

$18.61, together with the 50 cents left over from last week, leaves enough for me to buy tonight's bus ticket.

I do have a drawer of canned vegetables donated by a concerned lady, and a canister of Knox gelatin sent from the Left Coast by Latina Lynn, 30 ounces of good whisky and seven National Boh beers to round out the weeks supply. There is no way I consume all of this in a week, so next week's larder is already begun. My long term store of food, in the form of dried peas, beans and lentils are left over from last winter and should be eaten early this winter.

Himalayan Potpie
Cooking with Bryce

© 2016 James LaFond

I've grown wary of 25-cent burritos every day. I like them just as much as I did last week. But, I'm concerned about nutrition.

I searched in the fridge and saw the ground pork I cooked and drained last Thursday, or rather what is left, about a half-pound. When I open the lid it smells fine, so in it goes to the Pyrex pie pan.

For fresh vegetables I chose five jalapeno-stuffed olives and a clove of garlic that is as big as my thumb and cut them into fine slivers to give this repast a gourmet ambiance.

Then on goes three hefty shakes of the smoked parka/lime adobo.

Running low on paper plates and not wanting a mess, I dragoon the out-of-date corn tortillas and tear them up to form a spatter proof—as well as edible!—cover.

And, yes, Bryce is an actual gourmet chef, a former roommate and Green Party kind of guy, who has been gone for 2.5 years now. However, he did gift me a plastic salt grinder loaded with pink Himalayan salt, which will no doubt add some crucial micronutrient to this meal that might not be among the multitude of nutrients listed on the burrito package and which I might therefore be lacking. Crunch, crunch: salt from around the world graces the corn tortillas and into the microwave it goes.

I set it on dinner plate and only smelled it a little bit, so I'm hitting dinner plate again...

...At 1:56 its smelling good—like tortillas, like they weren't even stale!

At 42 this meal is smelling like a success—

Yes, slicing the tortillas and mixing them in helps absorb the traces of grease and should render cleanup easier. Eating as I post.

Thanks, Bryce.

Two Real Ghetto Gourmets
Cindy: Waiting Tables in Little Italy, Circa 2004

© 2016 James LaFond

I was a waitress at a very expensive and well-respected restaurant in Little Italy. The kitchen was filthy—disgusting. Two guys worked in the kitchen, Bryant, a stoner white boy, and Antonio—a ghetto-ass black dude. People complain about Little Italy now with all of the staff being Mexican. But what has changed—like it was "Italian" when you used to have potheads who lived off of Pop Tarts cooking your Chef's special? How about a chef period! I never ate a thing there. Sure, the guys in the kitchen wanted to date me, but I couldn't trust that. Say "no" or "maybe" one time too many and my lunch is going in the trashcan before it hits the griddle. Actually, the trash can would have been cleaner than the other surfaces in the kitchen—like these guys were going to clean?

We had a man who came in every day to get his stuffed shells for lunch, an older Italian man who totally hated blacks. It's a small place. You can see the cooks going from the kitchen to the bathroom and the cooks can hear you. It was just an old row house. So, after Mister Tummenello saw Antonio the first time, he would say, every time he sat down to order, "Is that nigger in the kitchen? I don't want that nigger touching my food."

I tried to get him to quiet down but they always heard. I'd come back to the kitchen and place the order and Antonio would say, "Did that old racist call me a nigger?"

I would play it down and say, "Look, he's like a hundred years old. Just let it go." I never stuck around to see what they did with his stuffed shells, but I can imagine. They had code words for customers they hated, and I don't know what they meant by "special sauce" or "Memphis rub." I can imagine though, after what happened with this old Jewish lady. She wasn't real old, like forty-five—but I was eighteen. So I'm like horror stricken, like I'm going to look like that one day!

She ordered the fillet and it comes with a garnish of parsley and she freaked the hell out, started yelling that she couldn't have green stuff touching her food, that she wanted a new steak, "What kind of imbeciles do you have working in the kitchen," "What's the matter with you, simple girl", blah, blah, blah.

Of course, those two heard it all. So when I bring the fillet back and tell them she wants another, Bryant says, "Fuck that, rugby rub, coming right up," tilts the plate, and drop-kicks the fillet to Antonio. And these guys were good. It was like watching professional soccer. So you know they had kicked food around the kitchen a lot. The fillet even went into the drain trap under the sink, then gets kicked out of there and goes skidding cross the dirty floor. Finally, Antonio scoops it up with the toe of his shoe, pops it up, and kicks it with the same foot to Bryant, who catches the thing with his spatula and drops it on the griddle, about five seconds on each side, just enough to raise some steam and back on the plate it goes and I'm taking this God-awful steak out to this God-awful woman.

I just couldn't do it anymore. I was afraid of pissing them off, as ghetto as they were—would not even bring shit up like this to the owners—are you kidding me!

I got out of there none too soon, let me assure you of that!

I couldn't even stand to watch the lady take her taste. But she liked it and told me I could go do whatever it was I did when I wasn't getting orders wrong—and I felt a little less bad about the entire episode.

Honestly, if you eat in a restaurant, you're fucking insane. I'd rather pick berries on the side of the road.

www.ingramcontent.com/pod-product-compliance
Lightning Source LLC
Chambersburg PA
CBHW060236290526
45789CB00001B/76